Fiscal Policy in Transition

Forum Report of the Economic
Policy Initiative no. 3

Fiscal Policy in Transition

Forum Report of the Economic Policy Initiative no. 3

Contributors:
Fabrizio Coricelli
Università di Siena and CEPR

Marek Dąbrowski
CASE Foundation, Warsaw

Urszula Kosterna
CASE Foundation, Warsaw

Editors:
Lorand Ambrus-Lakatos
Central European University, Budapest, and CEPR

Mark E Schaffer
Heriot-Watt University

INSTITUTE FOR EASTWEST STUDIES
WARSAW • PRAGUE • BUDAPEST • KOŠICE
NEW YORK • KYIV • BRUSSELS

Centre for Economic Policy Research

The Centre for Economic Policy Research is a network of over 350 Research Fellows, based primarily in European universities. The Centre coordinates its Fellows' research activities and communicates their results to the public and private sectors. CEPR is an entrepreneur, developing research initiatives with the producers, consumers and sponsors of research. Established in 1983, CEPR is a European economics research organization with uniquely wide-ranging scope and activities.

CEPR is a registered educational charity. Institutional (core) finance for the Centre is provided by major grants from the Economic and Social Research Council, under which an ESRC Resource Centre operates within CEPR; the Esmée Fairbairn Charitable Trust; the Bank of England; the European Monetary Institute and the Bank for International Settlements; 20 national central banks and 40 companies. None of these organizations gives prior review to the Centre's publications, nor do they necessarily endorse the views expressed therein.

The Centre is pluralist and non-partisan, bringing economic research to bear on the analysis of medium- and long-run policy questions. CEPR research may include views on policy, but the Executive Committee of the Centre does not give prior review to its publications, and the Centre takes no institutional policy positions. The opinions expressed in this report are those of the authors and not those of the Centre for Economic Policy Research.

2 May 1997

25–28 Old Burlington Street, London W1X 1LB, UK
Tel: (44 171) 878 2900
Fax: (44 171) 878 2999
Email: cepr@cepr.org

© Economic Policy Initiative, 1997

British Library Cataloguing in Publication Data
A Catalogue record for this book is available from the British Library

ISBN: 1 898128 30 8

Prepared and Printed by MULTIPLEX medway ltd, Walderslade, Kent.

Institute for EastWest Studies (IEWS)

The role of the Institute for EastWest Studies has remained constant since its founding in 1981: to help build a secure, prosperous, democratic, and integrated Europe. It does this as a transatlantic, multinational public policy network and think tank working to assist those who make policy in Europe, Russia, the Newly Independent States, and the United States. It seeks to overcome the divisive legacies of the twentieth century while creating a new order in Europe in which governments, the private sector, and non-governmental organizations work effectively together. The Institute is a non-profit organization, governed by an international Board of Directors and funded by foundations, corporations and individuals from North America, Europe and Asia.

In 1990, the Institute launched a major long-term cooperative venture in Central Europe, with a mandate to sponsor dialogue and cooperative research aimed towards building more secure relationships within and between the East and the West. Its steadily growing presence in the region includes centres in Prague, Budapest, Warsaw, Kyiv and Brussels, and the Foundation for the Development of the Carpathian Euroregion (FDCE) in Košice. With direct presence in the United States and Central Europe, liaison offices in other countries of the region, and activities conducted in Western Europe as well, the Institute occupies a unique strategic position between East and West.

The Institute's network of political, business and academic associates and its 60 staff in Central Europe and the United States contribute to economic, security and political aspects of IEWS programmes which include: Community Development and Democratic Institutions, European Security, European Integration, and Financial Sector Reform.

Institute for EastWest Studies
700 Broadway, 2nd Floor
New York, NY 10003
USA
Tel: (1 212) 824 4100
Fax: (1 212) 824 4149
President: John Edwin Mroz
E-mail: iews@iews.org

IEWS Warsaw Centre
Oboźna Street 7/32
00-332 Warsaw
Poland
Tel: (48 22) 826 8595, 827 0272, 828 2521
Fax: (48 22) 828 2520
Director: Andrzej Rudka
E-mail: warsaw@iews.org

Contents

List of Tables   ix
List of Forum Participants   xi
Foreword   xiv

1 Introduction   1
   Lorand Ambrus-Lakatos and Mark E Schaffer

2 Dynamics of Fiscal Developments During Transition   3
   Marek Dąbrowski
   2.1   General Picture   3
   2.2   Initial Destabilization Stage   4
   2.3   The Initial Stabilization/Liberalization Package   6
   2.4   The Stage of 'Secondary Fiscal Crisis'   9
   2.5   The Stage of Fiscal Consolidation   14
   Notes   14

3 Restructuring, Phases of Transition and the Budget   16
   Fabrizio Coricelli
   3.1   Introduction   16
   3.2   Transition   17
   3.3   Empirical Evidence on Fiscal Constraints and Feedback
          on the Speed of Transition   19
   3.4   Concluding Remarks   22
   Notes   23

4 A Comparative Analysis of Fiscal Policy in Selected Central European Countries 24
Urszula Kosterna
4.1   The Size of the Government and the Scope of Fiscal
       Redistribution   24
4.2   Structural Analysis of the Expenditure Side   28
4.3   Structural Analysis of the Revenue Side   33
Notes   38

5 Fiscal Policy: a Long-Term View 39
Fabrizio Coricelli
5.1   Sustainability of Fiscal Policy   39
5.2   The Size of Governments, Budget Deficits and Growth   43
Appendix   50
Notes   51

6 The Fiscal Policy Stance in Central and Eastern Europe in Comparison to European Union Countries 53
Urszula Kosterna
6.1   Fiscal Developments in EU Countries in an Historical
       Perspective   53
6.2   The Fiscal Situation of CEE Countries from the Point of View
       of Their Future Membership in the EU   57
6.3   The Structure of Budgetary Expenditures and Revenues   63
Notes   67

7 Conclusions and Recommendations 69
Lorand Ambrus-Lakatos and Mark E Schaffer
7.1   Introduction   69
7.2   General Conclusions and Recommendations   70
7.3   Accession Criteria   71
Note   73

References   74
Index   79

List of Tables

2.1 Adjustments of revenues and expenditures in selected post-communist
    countries during stabilization-liberalization stage. In percent of GDP   7
2.2 General government subsidies in the countries conducting a radical
    variant of stabilization. In percent of GDP   9
2.3 Investment expenditures of general government in countries
    conducting a radical variant of stabilization. In percent of GDP   9
3.1 Changes in government expenditures from 1989 to 1994. In percent
    of GDP   20
3.2 Changes in government revenues from 1989 to 1994. In percent
    of GDP   20
4.1 Revenues and expenditures of general government in Central
    European countries. In percent of GDP   25
4.2 The size of budgetary redistribution versus GNP/GDP level in
    12 European Union and 5 Central European countries in 1994   26
4.3 General government expenditures in Central European countries.
    In percent of GDP   29
4.4 General government revenues in Central European countries.
    In percent of GDP   35
4.5 Tax rates in Central European and European Union countries   36
5.1 Nominal government and operational (consolidated) deficit. In
    percent of GDP   42
5.2 Selected Countries in Transition: Simulated Growth Rates
    (Barro, 1991)   43
5.3 Developing Countries: Fiscal Deficits and Economic Performance
    Annual averages; in percent of GDP   45
6.1 Revenues, expenditures and general government budget balance in
    12 European Union countries. In percent of GDP   54

6.2 Maastricht criteria and fiscal performance of European Union
countries in 1994 and 1995   57
6.3 Government budget balance and public debt in CEE countries in
1994 and 1995   58
6.4 Broad money in EU and CEE Countries. Percentage share of GDP   60
6.5 General government expenditures in EU (1990) and CEE (1995)
countries. Percentage share of GDP   64
6.6 General government current revenues in EU and CEE countries.
Percentage share of GDP   66

Forum Participants

Mark Allen, *International Monetary Fund, Budapest*
Lorand Ambrus-Lakatos, *Central European University, Budapest, and CEPR*
Vladimir Benacek, *CERGE, Prague*
Erik Berglöf, *ECARE, Université Libre de Bruxelles, Stockholm Institute of Transition Economics and East European Economies, and CEPR*
Jorge Braga de Macedo, *Universidade Nova de Lisboa and CEPR*
Jonas Cicinskas, *Commission of the European Communities, Brussels*
Mitja Cok, *University of Ljubljana*
Fabrizio Coricelli, *Università di Siena and CEPR*
László Csaba, *Kopint-Datorg Institute, Budapest*
György Csáki, *Hungarian Academy of Sciences, Budapest*
Janusz M Dąbrowski, *Gdańsk Institute for Market Economics*
Marek Dąbrowski, *CASE Foundation, Warsaw*
Daniel Daianu, *National Bank of Romania, Bucharest*
David Daly, *European Commission Delegation, Budapest*
Alain de Crombrugghe, *University of Namur*
Rumen Dobrinsky, *21 Century Foundation, Sofia*
Gyula Gaál, *Member of Parliament, Budapest*
Gancho Ganchev, *Ministry of Economic Development, Sofia*
Mitja Gaspari, *Ministry of Finance, Ljubljana*
Florin Georgescu, *Ministry of Finance, Bucharest*
Maciej Grabowski, *Gdañsk Institute for Market Economics*
Antal Gyulavári, *National Bank of Hungary, Budapest*
László Halpern, *Institute of Economics, Budapest, and CEPR*
Stephen Heintz, *IEWS, Prague*
István Hetényi, *Ministry of Finance, Budapest*
Andriej Illarionov, *Institute of Economic Analysis, Moscow*

Leszek Jasiński, *European Integration Committee, Warsaw*
Morten Jung-Olsen, *Commission of the European Communities, Brussels*
Eugen Jurzyca, *Center for Economic Development (CED/CPHR), Bratislava*
Béla Kádár, *Member of Parliament, Budapest*
Evzen Kocenda, *CERGE, Prague*
János Köllö, *Hungarian Academy of Sciences, Budapest*
Jenö Koltay, *Hungarian Academy of Sciences, Budapest*
Janez Kopac, *Member of Parliament, Ljubljana*
Urszula Kosterna, *CASE Foundation, Warsaw*
Josep M Lloveras, *Commission of the European Communities, Brussels*
Millard Long, *World Bank, Budapest*
Vassilis Maragos, *European Commission Delegation, Sofia*
Anton Marcincin, *Center for Economic Development (CED/CPHR),
    Bratislava*
Kálmán Mizsei, *Hungarian Export-Import Bank Ltd, Budapest*
Jan Mladek, *Czech Institute of Applied Economics, Prague*
Tsuneo Morita, *Nomura Research Institute, Budapest*
John Edwin Mroz, *IEWS, New York*
László Muraközy, *Debrecen University*
Amir Naqvi, *European Commission Delegation, Ljubljana*
Judite Neményi, *National Bank of Hungary, Budapest*
David Newbery, *Department of Applied Economics, University of
    Cambridge and CEPR*
Gábor Oblath, *Kopint-Datorg Institute, Budapest*
Eva Ozsvald, *Hungarian Academy of Sciences, Budapest*
Gaspar Pal, *Research Institute for Finance, Budapest*
Tibor Palankai, *Institute of World Economics, Budapest*
Michael Patai, *Institute of World Economics, Budapest*
Joan Pearce, *Commission of the European Communities, Brussels*
Pete Pétar, *Hungarian Academy of Sciences, Budapest*
Constanze Picking, *CEPR*
Richard Portes, *London Business School and CEPR*
Alicja Potocka, *IEWS, Warsaw*
Roberto Rocha, *World Bank, Budapest*
Märten Ross, *Bank of Estonia, Tallinn*
Jacek Rostowski, *Central European University, Budapest*
Andrzej Rudka, *IEWS, Warsaw*
Mark E Schaffer, *Heriot-Watt University*
Brigita Schmögnerová, *Member of Parliament, Slovakia*
András Semjén, *Hungarian Academy of Sciences, Budapest*
Erica Simo, *IEWS, Budapest*
Witold Skrok, *Ministry of Finance, Warsaw*
Eugene Spiro, *IEWS, Budapest*

Pawel Stepanek, *Ministry of Finance, Prague*
Theodor Stolojan, *World Bank, Washington DC*
István Székély, *United Nations Department of Economic and Social Information and Policy Analysis, New York, and National Bank of Hungary, Budapest*
Tamás Tétényi, *Ministry of Finance, Budapest*
Alexander T Tomov, *21 Century Foundation, Sofia*
Ádám Török, *Hungarian Academy of Sciences, Budapest*
Marina Varga, *European Commission Delegation, Budapest*
Radu Vasile, *Member of Parliament, Romania*
Drahomira Vaskova, *Ministry of Finance, Prague*
Janos Vincze, *National Bank of Hungary, Budapest*
Paul Wachtel, *IEWS, New York*
Stephen Yeo, *CEPR*

Foreword

Launched towards the end of 1995 by the Centre for Economic Policy Research and the Institute for EastWest Studies, the Economic Policy Initiative comprises a programme of interrelated activities designed to strengthen and 'multilateralize' the public policy process in the Associated Countries (ACs) and assist their preparation for accession to the EU. The Initiative operates in seven EU Associated countries – Bulgaria, the Czech Republic, Hungary, Poland, Romania, the Slovak Republic, and Slovenia – where local partner institutes coordinate activities within their own country. Additionally, participants from Estonia, Latvia, Lithuania, Russia, and Ukraine are involved as observers.

As part of the Initiative, CEPR and IEWS established the Central European Economic Policy Forum. Here decision-makers from the private sector, senior policy-makers and researchers from both Central and Western Europe meet to discuss key economic policy issues and put forward focused recommendations to the governments of the ACs, the EU and its member states. The Forum meets semi-annually and considers the report of an expert working group, who incorporate into their report the comments and recommendations of the Forum participants for publication. The first Forum Report in the series focused on 'Banking Policies in the ACs', following the conference held at the College of Europe, Warsaw, in January 1996. A pamphlet containing its main analysis and recommendations and a single-page summary of the proposals is also available. The second Report is based on presentations of the second Forum on 'Coming to Terms with Accession', held at Université Libre de Bruxelles in June 1996. This, the third Report in the series focuses on presentations of the third Forum on 'Fiscal Policy in Transition', held in Budapest on 16/17 November 1996 with the Institute of Economics of the Hungarian Academy of Sciences.

We gratefully acknowledge financial support for the Initiative provided by the Ford Foundation, the Pew Charitable Trusts and the EU's Phare

Programme. Any opinions expressed in this Report are those of the authors and not those of CEPR, IEWS or the funding organizations. Neither CEPR nor IEWS take institutional policy positions. The funding organizations do not give prior review to the publications within the project, nor do they necessarily endorse the views expressed therein. Lastly, we thank various individuals who have contributed to the success of this project: first and foremost, Constanze Picking and Andrzej Rudka for their energy and determination in the management of the Initiative; Jenö Koltay, Eva Ozsvald and their colleagues at the Institute of Economics for organizing the Forum; Alicja Potocka for support during the organization of the Forum; James MacGregor for guiding the Report through production; Iwona Ławniczak-Iwanowska and Lorraine Forsdyke for secretarial assistance in the administration of the project; and last, but not least, the authors and editors, whose effort and cooperation in working under a very tight time schedule has been vital.

John Edwin Mroz
Richard Portes
2 May 1997

1

Introduction

Lorand Ambrus-Lakatos and Mark E Schaffer

Fiscal policy has turned out to be one of the most difficult components of transition policy, reflecting problems that arise in other areas of post-Communist stabilization. Whenever countries were not able to realise a consistent policy of economic liberalization, eliminate open and hidden subsidies, introduce hard budget constraints for state enterprises, inhibit interventionist inclinations, carry out tax reforms, improve the efficiency of tax administration and the entire fiscal apparatus, and launch reforms of the social welfare system and social services, etc., it meant that they would likely face some sort of deep, fiscal crisis. Fiscal crises usually lead to higher inflation, and in some extreme cases hyperinflation. This situation has an analogy in politicsevelopment; comparisons between these countries; the relationship between fiscal policy and the overall success of economy-wide restructuring; the role of fiscal policy in macroeconomic stabilization; and the wider European context. This is a succinct yet comprehensive account of the fiscal situation in Central and Eastern Europe, of interest to anyone concaid that the share of public spending in gross domestic product (GDP), the degree of stability of the overall system of public finances (including local budgets and extra-budgetary funds and institutions), and the size of the public debt constitute synthetic indicators of the quality of the transition process and of development perspectives in a given transition economy.

The purpose of this report is to provide an analysis of the key fiscal policy problems under transition, with special attention to a group of five Central and Eastern European (CEE) economies (the Czech Republic, Hungary, Poland, Slovakia and Slovenia). These countries are considered to be the most advanced in the transition to a market economy and as having the best chance to become members of the European Union (EU) at the beginning of the next decade. Just as launching market-oriented economic reforms and implementing them with speed and diligence was the priority task just after the collapse of the Communist system, accession to the EU seems to be the biggest political and economic challenge for the CEE countries in the coming few years. Naturally, fiscal policy will be of key importance in the integration process because it not only serves as a pivotal macroeconomic indicator but it reflects, as emphasised above, the quality of the overall transition process.

The structure of the report is as follows. Chapter 2, by Marek Dąbrowski, provides a dynamic (historical) analysis of the evolution of fiscal policy problems under subsequent stages of transition. In Chapter 3, Fabrizio Coricelli examines how, in particular, the task of restructuring the economy affected the state of the budget. Urszula Kosterna, in Chapter 4, compares the fiscal policy patterns and problems recently experienced by the individual CEE countries, i.e., after having completed the first stage of transition. In Chapter 5, Coricelli examines long-term considerations and Kosterna in Chapter 6 offers a juxtaposition of the fiscal policy patterns in the CEE and EU countries. In Chapter 7, we (the editors) discuss some of the report's conclusions and recommendations and consider how to link fiscal reforms and targets to the accession of the CEE countries to the EU.

2

Dynamics of Fiscal Developments During Transition[1]

Marek Dąbrowski

2.1 General Picture

Before starting the analysis of fiscal policy during transition, it is necessary to say a few words about the different transition strategies adopted by various post-communist countries. The categorization proposed below is based on a qualitative analysis[2] of the following three factors (Dąbrowski, 1996a):

- The progress achieved in the three main areas of transition process: (i) macroeconomic stabilization, (ii) liberalization and institutional changes, and (iii) privatization and restructuring (i.e., the extent to which a given country has adopted the standards existing in developed market economies).
- The speed of the changes adopted.
- The comprehensiveness and internal consistency of the reform package.

As a result, we arrive at six categories of transition countries:

1. The former German Democratic Republic, which, beginning on 1 July 1990, underwent almost immediate transformation based on the Agreement on Monetary, Economic and Social Union, supplemented by the Unification Treaty of October 1990. In practice, this case represented a total institutional 'absorption' of the former GDR by the Federal Republic of Germany.
2. The first generation of fast reformers (Poland, Czech Republic, Slovakia, Hungary, Slovenia, Albania).
3. The second generation of fast reformers (Estonia, Latvia, Lithuania, Kyrgyzstan, Moldova, Croatia, Macedonia).

4. The third generation of fast reformers (Armenia, Kazakstan, Georgia).
5. Slow and inconsistent reformers (Romania, Bulgaria, Russia, Ukraine).
6. The remaining countries, which suffer from armed conflicts (New Yugoslavia, Bosnia and Herzegovina, Azerbaijan, Tajikistan) or have halted the reform process because of political reasons (Belarus, Uzbekistan, Turkmenistan).

Both the fiscal situation of post-communist countries and the nature of their fiscal problems have changed in the course of transition process. One can 'stylize' the following four-stage fiscal policy scenario which most of the countries that succeeded in completing the first transformation stage—the first generation of fast reformers—went through:[3]

1. Macroeconomic destabilization (including fiscal destabilization) in the period directly preceding the launching of political and economic transition.
2. Initial macroeconomic stabilization connected with liberalization.
3. Secondary, post-stabilization fiscal crisis.
4. Fiscal consolidation.

2.2   Initial Destabilization Stage

The post-communist countries inherited from the command system a number of serious economic problems including fiscal problems. The most serious of these are, first, full or almost full nationalization, which 'squeezed' individual savings and directly or indirectly limited private economic activity. The natural consequence was the practice of financing investment mainly from budgetary and quasi-budgetary resources (off-budget funds, funds collected by bodies such as associations of enterprises, targeted central bank credits), and only secondarily from profits of enterprises and private savings collected by the state savings bank and redistributed through the banking system for development processes steered by the state.

Second, these economies inherited huge structural distortions resulting from the creation of strong monopolistic structures, autarkic trade policy, administrative regulation of prices and centralized investment decisions. Currency inconvertibility, state price control, trade restriction and state monopoly in foreign trade—all these factors led to the isolation of these economies from the international market. The budget played here the role of the main buffer allowing the state to run an artificial structure of prices which differed both from the structure of production costs and from the structure of the (international) market.

The third of these inherited fiscal problems was the substantial social obligations of the state in comparison with the economic development level reached by those countries (Sachs, 1995a).

All these specific characteristics of the command system led to a very high level of fiscal redistribution. Along with decreasing allocative effectiveness of the centrally-planned economy and gradual weakening of financial discipline (as a result of gradual political liberalization of the communist system), fiscal disequilibrium started to constitute a growing problem for the Central and East European (CEE) economies, particularly in 1980s. Fiscal disequilibrium led almost automatically to a monetary disequilibrium since the fiscal or quasi-fiscal deficit was financed by monetary emission. This led, in turn, to inflationary pressure, either in a hidden (shortage of goods) or open (price increases) form; sometimes both phenomena existed together. Foreign credits appeared to be an alternative method of financing the actual deficit of the public sector. In the case of most East European countries (Poland, Bulgaria, Hungary, Yugoslavia, and at the end of the 1980s, the USSR), this led to enormous external indebtedness.

If we look at the above list of legacies of the centrally-planned economy, we can point to them as the sources of permanent fiscal tensions. More detailed historical analysis reveals, however, some differences. Whereas centralized investment and structural distortions were rooted in early stages of socialist industrialization programmes (central allocation of resources, administrative prices and state monopoly in foreign trade), the social part of the heritage of the previous system is of a later origin. It was connected with the partial liberalization of the communist regime after Stalin's death, along with growing social dissatisfaction (the bloody events in Berlin in 1953, Poland in 1956 and 1970, Hungary in 1956, and the Prague Spring of 1968). Post-Stalinist communist leaders (Khrushchev and Brezhnev in the USSR, Kadar in Hungary, Ulbricht and Honecker in GDR, Husak in Czechoslovakia, Gierek and Jaruzelski in Poland) began to try to attract social support for their governments. The biggest jump, however, in social spending was recorded at the very end of the communist regimes, when the political establishment tried dramatically to buy electoral support. The most spectacular explosion of welfare spending and wages occurred in Poland in 1987–9 and in the USSR in 1990–1.

Governments also lost control over state-owned enterprises (SOEs) and their finances (especially wages) as the result of the incompleteness of 'socialist market' reforms that dismantled, to some extent, the traditional discipline of central planning, and offered no consistent solution in exchange. The growth of state enterprise autonomy in wage determination (indispensable for the creation of a more aggressive system of financial incentives for employees and management), coupled with a lack of adequate interest in profit, led to a decline in profit and budgetary revenues. Additionally, the level of wages paid in the enterprise sector affected—through informal and formal 'indexation'—the level of wages in the budgetary sphere, pensions, and other social contributions financed from the budget or extra-budgetary funds.

Even more harmful was a gradual and selective price liberalization, which led to a growing gap between market prices and administratively determined or regulated prices, where subsidies, tax exemptions, or other forms of financial compensation for producers were necessary. Since the goods and services sold at controlled prices represented—due to their great political sensitivity—a large share in overall market turnover, it led to an increase in subsidies and a decline in budgetary revenues.

Thus, slow and poorly coordinated price liberalization brought not only fiscal destabilization but also contributed to the increasing inflationary expectations, and, therefore, increasing money velocity. Precisely this happened in Poland in 1987–9 and in the USSR in 1989–91, where the problem of price liberalization was a subject of long public discussion. The destabilizing influence of gradual and inconsistent reforms in the late stage of socialism was additionally strengthened due to the weakness, and sometimes disintegration, of the socialist state (the case of the USSR, and of Yugoslavia in 1990–1).

Only Czechoslovakia, Hungary and the GDR avoided serious fiscal crisis at the beginning of transition period; however, even in these countries (especially in Hungary) macroeconomic equilibrium was far from ideal.

2.3   The Initial Stabilization/Liberalization Package

The experience of approximately 30 countries undergoing the transition process from plan to market reveals that macroeconomic stabilization is a necessary (although, however, insufficient) condition for achieving progress in other areas of transformation (see Balcerowicz and Gelb, 1995; Balcerowicz, 1994; de Melo, Denizer and Gelb, 1996; Dąbrowski, 1996a). Since a large fiscal and quasi-fiscal deficit constitutes a main source of macroeconomic instability at the very beginning of transition, an anti-inflationary programme must be directed to the elimination or reduction of that deficit. The 'standard' set of measures for doing so includes the following:

1. The elimination or substantial reduction in consumer and producer subsidies.
2. Cuts in other government expenditures (mainly investment and defence spending).
3. The reduction of tax exemptions and increases in tax rates or the introduction of additional emergency taxes if necessary.

4. The elimination of central bank quasi-fiscal spending (mainly in the form of a negative real interest rate, differentiated exchange rates and credits directed to particular sectors of the economy).

Measures listed in items 1, 3 and 4 are impossible without price liberalization. This in turn, because of the conditions of extensive monopolization prevailing in most of the post-communist economies at the beginning of transition, means external liberalization of the economy is needed.

Countries which achieved fundamental macroeconomic stability by 1995 (i.e., inflation below 30% per annum) enjoy a relatively low budget deficits. Only two out of ten countries representing this group (Albania and Hungary) had deficits exceeding 3% of GDP. Albania has received considerable external assistance in the form of foreign grants and concessionary loans (as has Moldova, which had inflation on the level of 30.2% in 1995). Hungary, as mentioned earlier, never went through pre-transition destabilization, and, thus, did not have to introduce strict stabilization measures. All adjustment activities related to budgetary expenditures in 1991–3 turned out, however, to be insufficient. This is why Hungary is the country that suffers most severely from the so-called secondary fiscal crisis (see below).

Individual countries differ from each other in the scale and detailed path of fiscal adjustments. Table 2.1 shows two paths of fiscal adjustment. The first path is represented by Czechoslovakia, Bulgaria and Albania, which maintained the classical command system until the very end of communist regime. In 1989, these three countries registered the highest share of expenditures in GDP (from 57.0% of GDP in Albania upto 72.3% in Czechoslovakia). In subsequent years they recorded a significant decline both in expenditures and revenues. In Czechoslovakia, however, the fall in expenditures and revenues was very similar, resulting in a low budget deficit. In Bulgaria and Albania, the decline in revenues significantly exceeded the decrease in expenditures; thus, the budget deficit increased. In both countries, the fall in real GDP was much stronger than in Czechoslovakia, meaning in fact a more dramatic decrease in real expenditures, and an even more substantial drop in real revenues.

Concerning Hungary and Poland, the economic systems of both countries were in 1989 much more decentralized, and both the scope of administered

Table 2.1   Adjustments of revenues and expenditures in selected post-communist countries during stabilization-liberalization stage. In percent of GDP

Country	Period of time	Expenditures	Revenues
Czechoslovakia	1989–91	−15.2	−14.5
Poland	1989–90	−9.1	+1.4
Hungary	1989–90	−3.5	−1.6
Bulgaria	1989–92	−16.2	−21.5
Albania	1990–92	−14.0	−26.5

Source: IMF *World Economic Outlook*, October 1994, Tables 14 and 15; de Melo, Denizer, and Gelb (1995), Table 8; World Bank PRD database; and author's estimates.

prices and subsidies as well as price distortions were smaller. The Hungarian economy was more market-oriented and better balanced in fiscal and monetary respects than the Polish economy. In 1988–9, Poland experienced a substantial drop in the share of revenues in GDP and a slight fall in the share of expenditures in GDP (Bratkowski, 1993; Bratkowski et al., 1995). In 1989, at the starting point, Hungary had a much higher share of expenditures of general government (61% of GDP) than Poland (48.9%), which would resemble the situation typical for the countries with a highly centralized version of the planned economy (see above). In 1989, the share of subsidies in Hungarian GDP (12.1%) was, however, lower than the Polish share (12.9%), not to mention the Bulgarian and Czechoslovakian shares (15.5% and 25%, respectively). In 1989, in comparison with Polish budget, the Hungarian budget had a higher share of the following expenditures:

- expenditures for goods and services (20.5% of GDP in Hungary and 10.2% of GDP in Poland), i.e., financing the budgetary sphere;
- debt service expenditures (2.4% and 0%, respectively);
- social security benefits expenditures (14.4% and 11.2%, respectively);
- capital expenditures (6.6% and 3.3%).

A lower initial share of subsidies in GDP, and in the case of Poland, a lower share of budgetary expenditures and revenues in GDP as well, resulted in both countries (Hungary and Poland) following a less dramatic fiscal adjustment than Czechoslovakia, Bulgaria and Albania. In 1989–90, as far as Hungary is concerned, the adjustment path consisted in relatively slight cuts both in general government expenditures (by 3.5% of GDP) and revenues (by 1.6% of GDP). Consequently, Hungary went from a slight deficit of general government (−1.4% of GDP in 1989) to a negligible surplus (+0.5% of GDP).

Poland, where in 1989 the deficit of general government amounted to 7.5% of GDP, was on the edge of hyperinflation in the second half of 1989. Therefore, Poland had to make deeper and more asymmetric adjustments than Hungary, lowering expenditures by 9.1% of GDP in 1990 (at the same time, there was a substantial fall in GDP) and increasing revenues by 1.4% of GDP. As a result, in 1990 a general government surplus of 3.0% of GDP was achieved.

Available statistical data allow us to examine only two items on the expenditure side, i.e., subsidies (see Table 2.2) and capital expenditures (see Table 2.3).

The most significant reduction of subsidies was made by Czechoslovakia (by 20% of GDP in 1989–92)—the country that had also had the highest starting level (25% of GDP). Czechoslovakia was followed by Albania (a reduction by 18.1% of GDP in 1991–3, with a starting level of 20.3% in 1991), Bulgaria (13.7% of GDP in 1989–92, although in 1993 an increase of 3% of

Table 2.2   General government subsidies in the countries conducting a radical variant of stabilization. In percent of GDP

Country	1989	1990	1991	1992	1993	Changes
Czechoslovakia	25.0	16.2	7.7	5.0	–	–20.0[a]
Poland	12.9	7.3	5.1	3.3	2.2	–10.7[b]
Hungary	12.1	9.6	8.0	5.8	4.8	–7.3[b]
Bulgaria	15.5	14.9	4.2	1.8	4.8	–13.7[a]
Albania	8.3	15.7	20.3	8.2	2.2	–18.1[c]

Notes: a – 1989–92; b – 1989–93; c – 1991–93.

Source: IMF *World Economic Outlook*, October 1994.

Table 2.3   Investment expenditures of general government in countries conducting a radical variant of stabilization. In percent of GDP

Country	1989	1990	1991	1992	1993
Czechoslovakia	8.5	6.9	8.4	11.3	–
Poland	3.3	2.8	2.2	1.7	1.5
Hungary	6.6	4.7	6.2	8.1	6.2
Bulgaria	5.5	3.1	2.0	2.8	1.9
Albania	29.3	18.8	6.1	4.3	7.7

Source: See Table 2.2.

GDP was registered), Poland (10.7% of GDP in 1989–93) and Hungary (7.3% of GDP within the same period).[4] It is worth repeating that the drop in subsidies was accompanied by a slump in GDP, and therefore, the decrease in overall real subsidies was even greater than the fall in their share in GDP. In 1993, the level of subsidies in Poland and Albania amounted to 2.2% of GDP, while in Hungary, the Czech Republic and Slovakia, they amounted to 4–5% of GDP.

As far as capital expenditures are concerned, there is no uniform trend. Albania, with a record level in 1989 (29.3% of GDP),[5] had by 1992 made the greatest relative reduction in these expenditures, which were down to 4.3% of GDP. In 1993, however, they increased to 7.7% of GDP. Bulgaria and Poland, beginning from a much lower level (5.5% and 3.3% of GDP respectively, in 1989), recorded a steady decline in capital expenditures (in Bulgaria, there was a temporary increase in 1992), while adopting a 'milder' trajectory than Albania's. In Czechoslovakia and Hungary, after a temporary and slight drop in 1990, the share of capital expenditures in GDP increased over the following years.

2.4   The Stage of 'Secondary Fiscal Crisis'

The improvement of the fiscal balances, resulting from radical adjustment activities at the very beginning of transition process, has not turned out to be sustainable. A majority of the post-communist countries that succeeded in the second stage experienced a secondary (post-stabilization) fiscal crisis shortly thereafter. The most important concrete reasons for the secondary fiscal crisis are the fall in budgetary revenues (particularly from enterprise income tax) and the increase in social spending.

Table 4.4 (see Chapter 4) shows a downward trend of revenue from the enterprise profit tax in all the CEE countries apart from Slovenia (where this tax has always been of minor importance). A rapid drop in average enterprise profitability is the basic reason.[6] Some reasons for that drop include:

- the withdrawal of direct and indirect subsidies and elimination of the 'duplication effect' (see Barbone and Marchetti, 1995) related to them, i.e., taxation of previously granted subsidies;
- an increase in domestic and external competition, and thus reduction of monopolistic profits;
- a weakening of SOE motivation to earn profits due to a temporary systemic and ownership vacuum;[7]
- a tendency to hide profits both in the private and state sectors as a form of tax avoidance (also a pre-privatization tactic in a part of the state sector);
- the elimination of so-called 'paper profits' as result of successful disinflation.

The last element seems to play a key role in all countries which were overcoming high or very high inflation. The large share of tax proceeds in GDP in Poland in 1990, and then their rapid decrease (in spite of the fact that effective tax rates remained unchanged) can serve as an example.[8]

In most countries, a drop in relative proceeds from enterprise profit taxes was partially compensated by increases in personal income taxes (this includes taxes on profits derived from economic activity conducted by physical persons). This effect was particularly dramatic in Poland, where, in 1992, with the introduction of the Personal Income Tax Act, a jump in budgetary proceeds from this tax was registered (from 5.8% of GDP in 1991 to 8.9% in 1992, and to 9.7% in 1993).

In contrast to corporate income tax, proceeds from turnover taxes, VAT and excise taxes either did not fall in relation to GDP (except for an initial period of price deregulation in several countries), or decreased on a smaller scale (see Table 2.4). The CEE countries that replaced the traditional turnover tax with VAT (Hungary in 1988, Slovenia and Croatia in the 1990s, the Czech and Slovak Republics at the beginning of 1993, and Poland in the second half of 1993) show a higher level of indirect tax proceeds than those countries that did not introduce any reforms. In addition, proceeds began to grow immediately when the reforms were implemented. This demonstrates the higher tax efficiency of the VAT in comparison with the traditional turnover tax.

The decline in GDP constituted an additional dramatic factor, worsening the fiscal situation in this stage of the transition. Thus, transition countries were faced not only with a substantial decline in the share of budgetary revenues in GDP, but also with an even greater decline in overall real revenues.

Most revenue sources are correlated with GDP, while the same cannot be said for expenditures. Most of them are more or less fixed (e.g., payments to government employees, public debt servicing or welfare spending). When GDP declines the share of the fixed expenditure in GDP can be expected to grow. In practice, in the case of social programmes, most of the post-communist countries were not only unable to reduce their commitments in this area, but also had to face new requirements and challenges, connected mainly with the direct and indirect effects of unemployment. For example, a rapid growth in the number of pensioners was a side-effect of the fall in employment. The withdrawal of many general subsidies for goods and services, the fall in registered employment and real wages, and the termination of social functions provided by state enterprises for their employees, have caused an increase in the demand for social welfare payments.

Moreover, the ineffectiveness of systemic solutions in the field of social policy inherited from the command system and/or created hastily in the first stage of transformation (often under the pressure of the first democratic election campaigns) have led to the expansion of welfare spending (see Table 4.3). The biggest problems have resulted from overly liberal unemployment and pension legislation. In the case of the latter, the excessive commitments have come from the following:

- A low retirement age and numerous entitlements to early retirement. In most post-communist countries pensioners can continue their work without any significant restrictions (this is usually a 'relic' of the era of labour deficits).
- Other branch and professional privileges (the use of preferential coefficients in the calculation of entitlements, bonuses, etc.).
- An overly short period of work used in calculating pension entitlements, which may lead to manipulation increasing the individual benefits.
- Non-equivalent (highly subsidized) pension schemes in the agricultural sector.
- Liberal definitions of entitlements and liberal rules for granting disability pensions.
- Poorly constructed and calculated principles of indexation of pension benefits, leading to a high replacement rate.

Any attempts to revise the operating principles of pension schemes (even elimination of obvious distortions) encounter strong political resistance (Sachs, 1995b), as well as the objection of constitutional courts (e.g., Poland and Hungary).

Apart from social obligation, there were also other sources for the increase in budget spending such as internal and external debt-servicing (Hungary, Bulgaria, Poland), so-called enterprise and bank restructuring (Hungary, Bulgaria), and sometimes various forms of subsidies (Bulgaria).

The problem of to what extent the secondary fiscal crisis was inevitable and how it could be avoided has been the subject of ongoing disputes. The supporters of gradual transformation initially blamed the excessive radicalism of economic stabilization and liberalization programmes (referred to as 'overshooting') for the secondary fiscal crisis (Nuti and Portes, 1993; Kołodko, 1991). According to them, so-called 'shock therapy' led to an excessive drop in output and enterprise profitability, and, thus, to a drop in budgetary revenues as well as excessive unemployment and costs of unemployment insurance benefits.

In Polish discussions, an argument concerning the alleged discrimination against the state sector (see Kołodko, 1992) has been put forward many times, although the followers of this idea have never presented any convincing evidence. Another argument has been related to the allegedly negative impact of privatization on economic activity and budgetary revenues (Kowalik, 1993).

The latter issue has also been a subject of the radical reformers' concern. In the beginning, the state sector seemed to show greater tax discipline than the private sector (particularly the thousands of small individual and family firms) and privatized sector. Moreover, rapid privatization and thus, restructuring, have been recognized as creating unemployment that leads to the growth of social spending. This has inspired discussions on the optimum pace of enterprise privatization and restructuring and transition as a whole (Roland, 1994; Aghion and Blanchard, 1993; Chadha and Coricelli, 1994).

On the other hand, the supporters of radical transformation have emphasized the negative influence on public finances of such factors as delay in fiscal reforms, over-expansion of social programmes, the results of the external shock coming from the collapse of the CMEA, and the lack of tight wage control in state enterprises (Dąbrowski, 1992; Gomułka, 1993; Crombrugghe, 1993; Bratkowski, 1993).

Now, from the perspective of the experience already accumulated with transition, the above controversy does not look as dramatic as a few years ago.

First, the examples of the Czech Republic, Slovenia and Estonia reveal that fiscal crises can be avoided. It must be noted that the fiscal policy scenario was different in each of the aforementioned countries. Estonia, having a relatively low level of general government revenues (31–35% of GDP in 1992–4) has been able to impose iron expenditure discipline, particularly in the area of welfare spending. In contrast, Slovenia, having very high welfare spending, has not only been able to maintain the earlier ratio of general government revenues to GDP, but even to increase it. To some extent, Slovenia has also benefited from the break-up of the Yugoslav federation, having been in the past an important net donor to other federal republics. All these reasons also apply in the case of the Czech Republic (i.e., maintenance of a relatively high level of tax revenues particularly from enterprises, disciplined welfare spending in comparison with Poland, Hungary and even Slovenia, and termination of earlier fiscal transfers to Slovakia).

Second, there is a correlation between the secondary fiscal crisis and the radical transition but it works in the opposite direction than suggested in the earlier discussion. The countries hardest hit by the crisis were Hungary, which in 1990–2 was seen by many commentators as a standard example of the gradualist strategy (which may be in some way reflected by the data in Table 2.2, showing the moderate pace of subsidy elimination),[9] and Bulgaria, where frequently changing governments very quickly detoured from the radical change path and began to 'soften' budget constraints for enterprise. Among the countries that avoided the secondary fiscal crisis are two exceptionally radical reformers, namely Estonia and the Czech Republic.

Third, a large drop in officially measured GDP turned out to be in fact unavoidable. Generally, however, it was smaller and shorter in the countries that adopted the most radical transformation variant (see de Melo, Denizer, Gelb, 1996; Dąbrowski, 1996a; EBRD, 1995; Balcerowicz and Gelb, 1995; Aslund, 1994). These were the first countries to return to the path of economic growth.

Fourth, any fears of the negative impact of overly rapid privatization on public finances have not been confirmed. The greater tax discipline of the state sector has turned out to be a transitory feature. State enterprises have quickly learnt from the private sector how to hide turnover and profits (or to transfer them out of the enterprise) and avoid taxes. Such practices have occurred on the greatest scale in the countries where the privatization of medium and large enterprises has been slow and SOEs have not faced hard budget constraints (Belarus, Ukraine, Bulgaria). In countries which completed the tax reform (Visegrad group and Baltic countries) private and privatized enterprises gradually seem to become better taxpayers than SOEs (see Antczak, 1996 for Poland).

The level of unemployment is not necessarily correlated with the speed of privatization process. Bulgaria was a slow privatizer but has a relatively high unemployment rate, whereas the Czech Republic and Estonia, which are fast privatizers, have relatively low unemployment. Moreover, expenditure for unemployment benefits and active labour market programmes, although important, are not the biggest items of social spending.

Fifth, the experiences of some Western countries (Sweden, Italy, Finland, France, and even the US) show that the problem of social and pension benefits guaranteed by the state is not exclusively typical for the countries undergoing the radical transition from plan to market.

2.5   The Stage of Fiscal Consolidation

In the case of radical reformers, a phase of transformation output decline lasted not longer than two (Poland) or three years (the Czech Republic, the Slovak Republic, Slovenia, Estonia, Latvia) from the beginning of the fundamental stabilization operation. Economic growth is usually connected with a proportional (or even greater) increase in revenues and not necessarily with a fully proportional rise in expenditures (the role of fixed expenses, discussed above);[10] thus, it should by itself help towards a fiscal recovery. In addition, long-term tax reforms (in particular, introduction of VAT and consolidated tax on personal incomes), improvement of the tax administration, and some minor adjustments of social expenditures start to bring positive results.

Movement from the third stage (secondary fiscal crisis) to the fourth stage (fiscal consolidation) is best exemplified by the Polish case, in which the budget deficit has been falling since the second half of 1993. The effects of economic growth (since 1992) and the aforementioned tax reforms have contributed to an improvement of the budget situation. To a lesser degree, this improvement was also due to some (rather mechanical) cuts in welfare spending and real salaries of government employees from 1991–3. The significant reduction of the budget deficit has resulted, above all, from an increase in the share of revenues in GDP as well as from the fast growth of GDP.

Symptoms of the gradual improvement of the budget situation can be observed in other countries which are advanced in the transformation process, such as Slovenia, Croatia, Estonia and the Czech and Slovak Republics. Hungary also presented in 1995 and 1996 a certain improvement in its fiscal balances in comparison with the period 1992–4.

The prospects for relative fiscal stability in the group of countries that are already at the fourth stage will depend on the intensity of the reforms of pension schemes, other segments of social policy, and basic areas of social services (health service and education). The fiscal situation of the countries that do not conduct these reforms quickly enough will mainly depend on their ability to maintain the high rate of economic growth. Any economic slump may easily lead to another serious fiscal crisis.

Notes

1. This chapter was written with the assistance of Ryszard Petru who prepared most of the statistical information. The author represents CASE (Center for Social and Economic Research), a private international research and policy advising institution in Warsaw, specializing in problems of the post-communist transition process. The author used extensively in this paper the results and conclusions of an earlier research project on 'The Fiscal Crisis in Central and Eastern Europe under Transition' carried out by CASE during the period January 1994–May 1996 and financed by the Ford Foundation. The chapter draws in particular on work done by Andrzej, S. Bratkowski, Jaroslaw Bauc, Pavel Stepanek,

Drahomira Vaskova, Vera Kamenickova, Vera Uldrichova, Milena Horcicova, Stefan Adamec, Antal Gyulavari, Judit Nemenyi, Lucjan T. Orlowski, Malgorzata Antczak, Marcin Luczynski, Krzysztof Polomski, Alain de Crombrugghe, Barbara Fakin, Luca Barbone, Hana Polackova, Jeffrey Sachs and Andrew Warner. Of course, the author of this chapter takes exclusive responsibility for its content, quality, and conclusions.

2. Obviously, this type of analysis includes a number of subjective elements, reflecting the differences in the level of the author's knowledge about the separate countries and his perception of the economic and political events that have occurred in those countries. Preparation of a more strictly quantitative ranking is beyond the agenda of this paper. Moreover, all attempts known to the author to prepare such a ranking based on a more formal quantitative analysis (e.g., the annual EBRD *Transition Report*; de Melo, Denizer and Gelb, 1996) provide a generally similar picture.

3. There are some exceptions which are discussed both in this paper and by the author in a more extensive study on dynamics of fiscal policy under transition (Dąbrowski, 1996b).

4. It is worth emphasizing that both Hungary and Poland reduced the share of subsidies in GDP in the preceding years due to partial price liberalization. In Poland, subsidies were cut substantially in mid-1989 in parallel with food price liberalization. In 1988–9, a fall in general government capital expenditures was also registered (Bratkowski et al., 1995).

5. In Albania in 1989 all enterprise investment spending was financed from the state budget.

6. In the case of Czech Republic and Slovakia a reduction of enterprise profit tax rates has also played a certain role.

7. The fiscal impact of the diversion of SOE profits to the wages of SOE employees was weakened, however, by revenues from the taxation of these (higher) wages (Schaffer, 1993).

8. These 'paper profits' or 'paper capital gains', are the result of the use of historical cost accounting by firms and have also often been observed in market economies experiencing inflation. Historical cost accounting means that sales revenue is accounted in prices at the time of sale, but the costs of the materials used in the products sold are accounted at (older) purchase prices. Inflation thus causes profits (sales minus costs of sales) to be artificially biased upwards, and although the upwards bias is an accounting artifact, it is still taxable. When inflation declines, profits and hence profit tax revenues subsequently fall as well. See Schaffer, (1993) for detailed estimates of this phenomenon in Poland in 1990–1 and Boulanger et al. (1995) for comparisons across a number of transition countries.

9. Looking retrospectively, however, over the period of seven years of transition and taking aside some official political rhetoric (the right-wing government in Hungary in 1990–4 generally opposed to the idea of 'shock therapy' and therefore used 'gradualist' rhetoric) Hungary must be categorized as a relatively fast reformer (see the classification in section 2.1).

10. In practice, it is not always possible to hold the expenditures down during the economic growth and increased budgetary revenues. Two political elements play a significant role here. These are, first, a willingness of different groups being the beneficiaries of the budget to participate in the results of economic growth, and second, government difficulty in opposing different pressure groups and carrying out unpopular reforms limiting the budgetary commitments. The fiscal crisis usually serves as the best argument for breaking the resistance of interest groups, whereas a good situation with respect to revenues softens the power of this argument.

3

Restructuring, Phases of Transition and the Budget

Fabrizio Coricelli

3.1   Introduction

The shift to a full-fledged market economy is bound to reduce the size and the scope of interference of the state in the economy in previously centrally-planned economies. Three main observations, however, qualify this obvious statement. First, the extent and the speed of the reduction in the size of the state is a policy option. Even after controlling for income levels, there is an extremely wide variation in the size of the state in market economies. Furthermore, the speed of the reduction may be crucial for the eventual success of the shift towards a market economy. Second, just as important as the size of the state is the composition of expenditures and taxes. In particular, the composition of expenditures and taxes should be evaluated in terms of its effects on the transition process. To give a simple example, expenditures for unemployment benefits paid to workers temporarily unemployed because of labour shedding in restructured firms differ sharply in their effects on transition from expenditures for subsidies to ailing state firms. Third, budget deficits are incomplete, and sometimes misleading, indicators of policy stance. Indeed, the evolution of budgetary flows is bound to be crucially affected by institutional changes.

Given the complexity of the transition process and the diversity in country experiences, a thorough treatment of fiscal issues during the transition is not feasible here. Nevertheless, it is useful to identify broad stylized facts and place them within a simple analytical framework.

First, abstracting from different end-points—possibly defined within the context of a full-fledged integration in the European Union—we need to specify the definition of transition. For the sake of simplicity we adopt a narrow definition of transition as the movement of resources from the state to the private sector, assuming the latter to be more efficient. The building of market institutions necessary to effect such transfer is another key aspect of transition and it involves important fiscal effects. Indeed, fiscal variables play the double role of symptoms of transition and of incentives for transition. Transition can be costly for fiscal accounts, as the shift of resources leads to transitory unemployment, exit from the labour force, and a fall in the tax base. At the same time, the level of unemployment benefits, pensions, taxes on state firms and private firms, and subsidies affect the incentives for the shift of resources across firms and sectors.

Focusing on 'positive' rather than normative aspects, we illustrate the dynamics of fiscal variables consistent with hypothetical successful and unsuccessful transition paths, whereby successful transition is defined as the shift of resources from state to private firms.

The analysis of this chapter thus assumes away a host of factors—including the role of short-term changes in output—that affect fiscal accounts. In this vein, recent models of transition (Aghion and Blanchard, 1993; Chadha and Coricelli, 1994) suggest that—*ceteris paribus*—budgetary pressures (worsening of fiscal accounts) are likely to be stronger along a successful path (Coricelli, 1996). This result should be interpreted as stating that, for a given situation, the decision of policy-makers in a given country to adopt a faster transition implies greater fiscal pressure.[1] Of course, if rapid transition takes place in countries characterized by much better fiscal systems and tax collection capacities, then actual deficits may be higher in slow reformers. Furthermore, the above statement holds for given short-term changes of output.

With these caveats in mind, we want to stress that fiscal constraints are a serious obstacle to successful reforms. Transition entails large social costs. Indeed, unemployment tends to rise, real incomes of a large part of the population fall and income inequality sharply rises. In turn, these costs imply fiscal costs directly (via unemployment benefits, social expenditures) or, indirectly, through pressure to soften the effects of transition on particular groups of the population.

3.2   Transition

Transition can be seen as a process of massive reallocation of resources across sectors and firms. Such a process contains elements of evolution—new firms emerge and absorb resources from the old, declining firms—and of policy design (firms are privatized, restructured or closed by state intervention).[2] The dynamics of the economy crucially depend on the weight of these elements.[3]

In the liberalized economy new economic activities emerge. Workers previously employed in state firms can now be employed in these growing new sectors. Simultaneously, state firms are subject to pressure to adjust to new conditions, which often means cutting costs and thus employment. Unemployment benefits are also introduced, allowing for the existence of unemployment.[4] Furthermore, early retirement has been widely used in several countries as a way to shed labour. Thus, retirement becomes an alternative option to employment, reducing the labour force and increasing social expenditures.

Three issues related to the labour market dynamics arising from the process of restructuring of the economy stand out:[5]

1. The behaviour of unemployment follows more closely the process of restructuring than the short-term behaviour of output. In fact, during the first stages of reform unemployment increases together with output growth. As new firms tend to be more productive than the old firms, output growth can be achieved even with a smaller number of employees. It is only after a while that new firms are able to absorb the labour force shed by declining firms. At that point, the relation between employment and output growth becomes negative.
2. A corollary of the first point is that the growth of the private sector is associated with higher unemployment in the early stages of transition.
3. The initial conditions on the capital stock that can be used in productive sectors, and thus the implied magnitude of restructuring needed, are crucial for the success of restructuring. A country with a large share of the capital stock built for activities that do not have a market opportunity in the new environment can only slowly absorb labour released from the old state sector in new activities. The initial costs of downsizing the state sector can be so high—in terms of fiscal costs or political opposition to reforms—that they can jeopardize the take-off of new private activities. The need to finance the fiscal cost of the contraction of state firms would put a heavy pressure on new firms, thus discouraging new investments.

The issues highlighted above have important implications for the dynamics of fiscal accounts.

First, more than the behaviour of aggregate output, it is the process of restructuring of the economy, with the attendant increase in unemployment, that plays a key role in the dynamics of the budget during transition.

Second, fiscal variables define the speed of transition. Indeed, a faster transition implies a sharper reduction in subsidies to state firms. As the sharper reduction in subsidies tend to be associated to initially higher rates of unemployment and/or exit out of the labour force, a faster transition implies initially a larger increase in expenditures for unemployment benefits and social expenditures.

Finally, social expenditures, such as unemployment benefits, play a dual role and have ambiguous effects on the transition process. Unemployment benefits, by affecting the reservation wage, may reduce the employment generated in the growing sectors, thus hurting restructuring. Unemployment benefits, however, determine as well the incentives for people to leave the old state firms. Similarly, social expenditures play a crucial role in the choice between employment and exiting from the labour force. Taking into account the risk of becoming unemployed, workers may find it attractive to retire. This option becomes even more attractive when workers are fired.

In sum, higher benefits may facilitate restructuring by reducing the incentives to maintain jobs in old state firms.

3.3   Empirical Evidence on Fiscal Constraints and Feedback on the Speed of Transition

During transition, the size of the public sector and its interference with economic life continued to be much larger than in market economies (see Chapter 4 of this report for a detailed discussion). This complicates the comparison of budgetary accounts over time, and their interpretation as indicators of fiscal policy (Tanzi, 1993a). The relation between budgetary developments and the characteristics and speed of restructuring reduce the informational role of the budget. Indeed, budget deficits may result from a strong commitment towards fast and far-reaching market reforms, rather than from a populist attitude, or from the maintenance of the status quo via large subsidies (Kornai, 1993; Tanzi, 1993a).

Using the EBRD classification of countries on the basis of the speed of reform, 'fast' reformers display a significantly higher ratio of unemployment rates to GDP growth.[6] This could be interpreted as an indication of the positive correlation between unemployment and structural change during the transition. The mechanism works through the effect of the sharp increase in unemployment and falling real wages on social expenditures. The latter, traditionally high in the previous regime of universal social protection, even increased in some cases.

More generally, we can identify the following pattern: fast reformers imposed harder budget constraints (measured as reduction in subsidies and taxation of firms), while compensating the losers of adjustment through higher social expenditure. Assuming the difference between profit tax and subsidies as an indicator of hardening of the budget constraint of firms, we find that between 1989 and 1994 in slow reformers this indicator fell by 1% of GDP, while in fast reformers it increased by 8% of GDP (see Tables 3.1 and 3.2).

Simultaneously, social security expenditures increased more in 'fast' than in 'slow' reformers (Table 3.1). This increase in expenditures appears the main cause of fiscal pressures, while the feared revenue collapse did not materialize in the more advanced reformers.

Table 3.1   Changes in government expenditures from 1989 to 1994. In percent of GDP

	1989	1994	Change 1989–94
Slow Reformers			
Social Security Benefits	10.0	11.8	1.8
Subsidies	10.6	2.5	–8.1
Capital Expenditure	11.6	3.0	–8.6
Total Expenditure	52.1	38.7	–13.4
Fast Reformers			
Social Security Benefits	13.9	22.5	8.6
Subsidies	20.7	7.4	–13.3
Cap Expenditure	7.9	8.4	0.5
Total Expenditure	68.5	61.6	–6.9

Source: Classification of fast and slow reformers based on EBRD classification (see text). Budget data from IMF, *World Economic Outlook*, October 1994 and October 1996.

Table 3.2   Changes in government revenues from 1989 to 1994. In percent of GDP

	1989	1994	Change 1989–94
Slow reformers			
Profit tax	15.3	6.4	–8.9
Wage tax and social security	13.4	14.3	0.9
Total revenue	55.4	34.7	–20.7
Fast reformers			
Profit tax	10.0	4.3	–5.7
Wage tax and social security	21.2	22.8	1.6
Total revenue	66.2	59.7	–6.5

Source: Classification of fast and slow reformers based on EBRD classification (see text). Budget data from IMF, *World Economic Outlook*, October 1994 and October 1996.

As noted above, the composition of expenditure is more meaningful than total expenditure. Indeed, total expenditures fell, on average, by the same proportion in the two groups. This shows the compensating movement of subsidies and social expenditures. In the fast reformer group, however, subsidies fell much more and social expenditure grew more than in the slow reformer countries. Thus, while fast reformers have absorbed in higher social security expenditures the impact of the cut in subsidies, slow reformers have opted for maintenance of higher subsidies, that, in the short run, may have moderated social expenditures. An alternative interpretation is that, given an overall budget constraint, slow reformers had less room for social expenditures. This, by itself, may have contributed to a slowdown of restructuring, because of the unattractiveness of income from being unemployed or out of the labour force.

Within social expenditures, the evidence is that the main pressures on public expenditure arose from pensions and other social benefits, rather than from unemployment benefits. The main source, however, of increased pension expenditure has generally been the increase in the number of pensioners leaving employment before the natural retirement age.[7] Thus, the increase in expenditure for pensions reflected largely the adjustment in the labour market.

Expenditures for social benefits were also largely determined by transfers to the unemployed that exhausted their entitlement to unemployment benefits.[8]

Thus, fast reformers displayed a sharp increase in pension expenditures that cannot be explained by demographic factors. Here we suggest that the increased pension expenditures are linked to labour market dynamics.

In 1994 the distribution of revenues in different tax and non-tax sources was similar in the two groups of countries (fast and slow reformers). Clear differences, however, emerge if one looks at the changes in various tax items that took place after reforms (Table 3.2). In the period 1989–94 one notes a significantly larger fall (four percentage points of GDP) of profit tax revenues in the slow reformer group.[9]

Thus, pressure—defined as tax payments as a ratio of their value added— on the tax paying firms, mainly state-owned enterprises, has been much higher in the fast reformer group. Furthermore, if one combines the tax pressure with the larger contraction in subsidies, it is apparent that the overall pressure has been much higher in fast reforming countries. This higher pressure may be considered as a key distinguishing characteristic of the faster speed of reform.

Two important qualifications are in order. First, in several countries the fall in revenues was concentrated in revenues other than enterprise taxes. Only in Bulgaria was the fall in profit tax the main cause of the overall collapse in revenues. Second, even within the group of fast reformers there were significant differences. What seems to emerge clearly, however, is that 'fast' reformers began the transition by putting strong pressure on state firms by reducing drastically subsidies and in most cases raising effective taxation.[10]

The important implication of the above analysis is that fast reforms implied fiscal costs. In some instances, especially in Hungary and Poland, as transition progressed and unemployment increased, there was pressure for slowing down transition. The loosening of the fiscal pressure came about mainly through the tolerated growth of tax arrears.[11]

To sum up, we find that fiscal pressures become stronger while the transition progresses, and they are more acute in the 'fast' reforming countries. Thus, demands on governments to slow down restructuring mount, as well as demands for compensating transfers to groups affected by reforms. Fast reformers could in a sense afford to compensate the losers. This, despite political setbacks, allowed reforms in these countries to be sustained over time. Dewatripont and Roland (1992) provide an analytical framework that rationalizes this phenomenon.

This does not mean that the way such transfers were designed and targeted were correct. In fact, Chapters 2 and 4 of this report show that often social transfers, as well as pension expenditures, were ill-targeted. Nevertheless, the above analysis points out that a key factor behind the increase in social expenditures and pensions may have been the successful process of restructuring of the economy, with its related dynamics of the labour market.

Early retirements at the outset of reforms, and the shift from unemployment benefits to social benefits after expiration of entitlement, explain a large share of the increase in pensions and social expenditures in advanced reforming countries.

One major problem with using pensions as a way of redistributing income towards generations adversely affected by transition, is that pensions generate an entitlement with respect to future transfers. Thus, the fiscal implications of what should be a temporary transfer are felt in the future, burdening pension systems already hardly sustainable because of unfavourable demographic factors. Rather than a generalized increase in pensions, the models discussed above suggest the importance of adequate transfer in the initial stages of transition to those adversely affected by the restructuring of the economy. Relatively high, but short-lived, unemployment benefits, and minimum pensions ensuring an income above the poverty line, are examples of policies consistent with the models. Moreover, as the key element of successful restructuring is the creation of jobs in private firms, expenditure in active labour market policies is likely to lead to high returns.[12]

Governments face an important trade-off. Excessively tight budget constraints may yield perverse effects, as they may slow down restructuring. Indeed, a fast decline of state enterprises would lead to adverse fiscal effects by increasing unemployment expenditures and, simultaneously, reducing the tax base. These effects are particularly strong when the taxation of state firms is still an important source of budgetary income.

Together with pressures arising from increasing income inequality and lobbying from specific interest groups, such as pensioners, fiscal constraints likely played a major role in the reform cycle observed in many CEE countries, and especially in determining the asymmetry between economic and political cycles. Examples of change over time in the speed of reforms are given by the continuing delay of privatization, as well as the widespread electoral failures of radical reformers.

3.4   Concluding Remarks

This chapter has stressed not only that fiscal indicators are imperfect indicators of policy stance towards reforms, but that budget tightening could generate perverse effects on the process of restructuring. Three main conclusions stand out. First, one can note a close connection between the speed of reforms, cuts in subsidies and the imposition of harder budget constraints, and the increase in social expenditures. Second, the increase in social expenditures was the main force behind worsening budget deficits. Such an increase was ill-conceived, as it was concentrated on pensions, with negative long-term consequences. Third, and relatedly, the need for initial transfers to losers to create support and, in fact, foster reforms should have been recognized, and appropriate schemes designed.[13] This has important implications for unemployment benefit policy, as well as for the design and reform of pension schemes.

Notes

1. These phenomena tend to affect countries asymmetrically, because of different initial conditions. The extent of the costs depends on the extent of the needed reallocation of resources and the endowment of physical and human capital that can be used in market activities.
2. Frydman and Rapaczynski (1994) use this characterization for the process of privatization.
3. Although it is a rough simplification, the adjustment following the initial output fall in economies in transition can be interpreted as the asymmetric dynamics of declining and growing sectors. Although the recovery of state firms deserves attention in some cases (most notably Poland), the distinction between private and state sectors captures a large part of the process (see Commander and Coricelli (1995) for an analytical and empirical discussion of these aspects).
4. With zero unemployment benefits a worker would accept staying in a firm as long as the benefits received for being employed, even if minimal, exceed the utility of leisure.
5. See Coricelli (1996) for a more detailed analysis.
6. The Czech Republic, Hungary, Poland and Slovakia belong to the fast reformer group, while Bulgaria and Romania belong to the slow reformer group. The classification is admittedly crude, and thus should be taken as merely indicative. The classification is based on indicators in three areas: (i) enterprise restructuring and privatization; (ii) market reform: price liberalization, competition both internal and external; (iii) financial sector reform (see EBRD, 1994, p. 11).
7. In Poland, for instance, the number of new pensions increased sharply in 1990/1, from 437,000 in 1989 to 653,000 in 1990 and 912,000 in 1991, while the number of people reaching retirement age was roughly constant at the level of 1989 (133,000 in 1989, 144,000 in 1990 and 138,000 in 1991) (Coricelli et al., 1995).
8. Coricelli (1995) reports evidence on the sources of the increased pension expenditure after reforms in economies in transition. Considering a regression line, based on a sample of 92 countries, as the level of expenditures 'justified' by demographic variables, it is shown that all the fast reformers are above the regression line, and, more important, they moved further away from the line after reforms. The only slow reformer country in the figure, Romania, is located below the regression line. Interestingly, a regression on pension expenditures and income per capita does not provide significant results. Thus, in a cross-country analysis, demographic factors are a better predictor than the income levels of the various countries.
9. It should also be noted that Bulgaria, one of the slow reformers, had a much higher level of profit tax before reforms (23% of GDP).
10. The relevant measure of fiscal pressure on state-owned firms is the taxation net of subsidies (Barbone and Marchetti, 1995).
11. See Schaffer (1995) for an analysis of tax arrears in transition economies.
12. See Burda and Lubyova (1995).
13. This issue is stressed as well by Dewatripont and Roland (1996).

4

A Comparative Analysis of Fiscal Policy in Selected Central European Countries[1]

Urszula Kosterna

4.1 The Size of the Government and the Scope of Fiscal Redistribution

One of the main features of centrally-planned economies was a very wide scope of budgetary redistribution (Chand and Lorie, 1992; Barbone and Marchetti, 1995)—a consequence of the philosophy of a 'command-and-distribute' economy in which the means of production were almost exclusively state-owned and prices were subject to administrative control. Therefore, market mechanisms did not exist and did not play any role in decision-making processes concerning production, consumption and the allocation of resources; these decisions were mostly centralized. Implementing the allocative function of the state consisted of re-directing existing resources to key industrial sectors (according to the preferences of the central planner). At the same time, a method of internal (intra-industrial) subsidization of certain types of manufacturing favoured by the central authorities was applied. The redistributive function (the mechanism for achieving an equitable income distribution) was exercised, at least theoretically, through government subsidies and transfers to housing, public transport, health-care, education and basic goods, as well as through an expanded system of social security. Therefore, apart from wages, which were insignificantly differentiated within the government sector, individuals received via their employer a number of non-wage benefits including access to subsidized goods and services: housing (i.e., flats built by an institution for its employees), institutional shops, holidays organized and partially or fully financed by the institution, etc. Such non-wage benefits composed a large portion of the total compensation package.

The process of a pro-market transformation of the economy requires a reduction in the state's role, with respect both to its direct participation in the

Table 4.1 Revenues and expenditures of general government in Central European countries. In percent of GDP

	1989	1990	1991	1992	1993	1994	1995	Change 1989–1995[a]
Poland								
Revenues	33.8	47.3	42.3	45.1	47.6	48.3	47.2	**+13.4**
Expenditures	39.9	43.6	48.9	51.8	49.9	50.5	49.8	**+9.9**
Hungary								
Revenues	59.2	57.6	51.9	55.2	54.9	54.6	51.3	**–7.9**
Expenditures	60.5	57.2	54.0	60.6	61.6	62.1	55.3	**–5.2**
Czechoslovakia								
Revenues	56.8	49.3	50.0					
Expenditures	58.9	49.5	52.2					
Czech Republic								
Revenues				48.2	51.4	51.2	50.4	**–6.4**
Expenditures				47.8	50.1	50.7	49.8	**–9.1**
Slovak Republic								
Revenues				46.1	44.2	46.4	47.9	**–8.9**
Expenditures				58.0	51.2	47.7	47.3	**–11.6**
Slovenia[b]								
Revenues	42.7	–	43.7	46.4	47.1	47.3	45.9	**+3.2**
Expenditures	40.6	–	41.1	46.2	46.8	47.5	46.2	**+5.6**

[a] The changes between 1989 and 1995 for the Czech and Slovak Republic and for Slovenia are approximations due to the incomparability of 1989 data: for the Czech and Slovak Republic these refer to Czechoslovakia; for Slovenia—to Yugoslavia.

[b] Data for 1989 refer to Yugoslavia.

Sources: MultiQuery Database: A Tool for Cross-Country Comparisons. Europe and Central Asia Region. The World Bank, Spring 1996. Data for Czechoslovakia and Yugoslavia: Government Finance Statistics. IMF, 1994.

economic process and to the scope of the redistribution of the gross national product (Tanzi, 1993b). This ought to make possible the transfer of decisions concerning the allocation of resources and the size and structure of consumption from the government to the private sector. Such a process can be described as a kind of state 'meta-interventionism' (Wojtyna, 1990), where the state deliberately acts to restrain its role in economic life and to re-introduce market mechanisms.

The relative size of government is usually measured as the ratio of government expenditure and revenue to GDP. Table 4.1 provides data illustrating the development of fiscal redistribution in five Central and East European (CEE) countries in transition.

Between 1989 and 1995, three countries reduced their ratio of general government expenditure to GDP. This ratio shrank by 11.6 percentage points in the Slovak Republic, 9.1 points in the Czech Republic and 5.2 points in Hungary.[2] In the other two countries the ratio grew—by 5.6 percentage points in Slovenia and 9.9 points in Poland. It is noteworthy, however, that despite this different evolution of the ratio of general government expenditure to GDP, the 1995 data indicate a convergence in this area: general government spending was close to 50% of GDP. Hungary, although successful in reducing

Table 4.2   The size of budgetary redistribution versus GNP/GDP level in
12 European Union and 5 Central European countries in 1994

Country	GNP per capita (USD, current exchange rate method)	GDP per capita (USD, purchasing power parity method)	Budget expenditures, share of GDP (%)	Budget current receipts, share of GDP (%)
Belgium	22870	20270	56.0	50.4
Denmark	27970	19880	62.5	58.3
France	23420	19670	55.5	49.9
Germany	25580	19480	49.4	46.6
Greece	7700	10930	49.9	35.8
Ireland	13530	13550	40.7	38.3
Italy	19300	18460	54.8	45.2
Luxembourg	39600	35860	52.7	54.0
Netherlands	22010	18750	55.9	52.1
Portugal	9320	11970	44.4	38.2
Spain	13440	13740	48.2	41.2
United Kingdom	18340	17970	42.6	36.3
EU 12			51.0	45.4
Poland	2410	5480	50.5	47.2
Hungary	3840	6080	62.1	53.8
Czech Republic	3200	8900	50.7	49.4
Slovak Republic	2250	6660	47.7	46.4
Slovenia	7040	6230	47.5	47.3

*Sources: WDR (1996); World Bank Atlas, 1996; Annual Economic Report for 1995,
European Economy No. 59, 1995; MultiQuery Database: A Tool for Cross-Country
Comparisons. Europe and Central Asia Region. The World Bank, Spring 1996.*

the scope of budgetary redistribution, still maintained the highest ratio of
general government expenditure to GDP (55.3%), 9.3 percentage points higher
than in Slovenia, which had the lowest ratio among the five Central European
countries.

Analysis of the evolution of the ratio of general government revenue to
GDP provides a similar picture. Again, the Czech and Slovak Republics and
Hungary reduced this ratio, while in Poland and Slovenia budgetary revenue
increased as a share of GDP. In 1995, the ratio varied from 45.9% in Slovenia
to 51.3% in Hungary.

Transition countries continue to maintain relatively high levels of
government spending (and revenue) as a share of GDP. A determination of the
optimal size of budgetary redistribution would always be arbitrary, since it is
linked to the debate on the state's role in the economy. There is, however, a
measure which indicates to some extent the potential of the economy to
maintain a large government—the level of economic development and wealth.
The observation of developed market economies, in an historical perspective,
points to the tendency of growth in the size of the public sector. This is often
described as Wagner's law, according to which government expenditure
increases at a faster pace than economic growth.

The causes of this phenomenon are not definitely known, and the attempts
to explain it mostly focus on political, social and institutional conditions

affecting the increase in government expenditure. Despite the reasons of the growth in spending, it is obvious that in a cross-country comparison, a higher level of development enables the maintenance of a larger government.

From the point of view of the future eastern enlargement of the European Union (EU), it is interesting to compare the level of budgetary redistribution in transition countries with the level seen in EU countries (Table 4.2).

The ratio of budget revenue to GDP in five CEE countries, in 1994, was higher than the average recorded for EU countries; transition economies, however, lag significantly in development. The level of wealth in post-socialist countries, as measured by the level of per capita GNP (current exchange rate method), is several times lower than that recorded in EU countries. Therefore, fiscal redistribution observed in relatively poor post-socialist countries must be considered excessive. Following the experience of European countries with long-lasting market structures, it could be concluded that the level of fiscal redistribution in post-socialist countries should amount at most to 30 to 40% of GDP (Wierzba, 1993; Gomulka, 1995a). Such levels were observed in EU countries in the 1950s and 1960s, i.e., over the period during which levels of per capita GDP were comparable with those currently observed in the CEE countries.

Per capita GDP reported at current exchange rates can be argued to be misleadingly low (Fakin and de Crombrugghe, 1995) in transition countries, but this concerns the poorest EU countries as well. Thus per capita GDP data based on purchasing power parity (PPP) does not really change the picture. The levels of wealth in CEE countries still do not reach those in the poorest EU countries where, however, the scope of fiscal redistribution is much lower than the average for 12 EU countries. This points to the need to continue reducing government expenditure, which would ease the fiscal burden of transition economies.

In addition, it should be emphasized that the situation in EU countries cannot be treated as a model—the level of budgetary redistribution taking place in these countries is estimated as excessive, and one specific fiscal policy aim (being pursued without success) since the beginning of the 1980s has been to reduce this level (see section 6.1 of this Report). West European countries, where the evolution of public finances has led to an excessive budgetary redistribution and crises of the welfare state, do not have to serve as a pattern for post-socialist countries to follow. According to Sachs and Warner (1996), the acceleration of the pace of economic growth—necessary to narrow the economic gap between CEE countries and the countries of developed market economies—is possible while patterning upon the experience of non-European economies, characterized by the fastest pace of growth over the last ten years (Hong Kong, Singapore, Malaysia, Taiwan, South Korea, Thailand, Chile, Mauritius). In all these countries the budgetary redistribution level is much lower than in EU countries (government expenditures in Hong Kong account for 14% of GDP, in Korea 17%).[3] Apart from the issues of the quality of government spending and the effectiveness of the government sector, a level of budgetary redistribution reduces income inequality, having a potentially negative impact on national saving and investment.

High levels of domestic saving are crucial for sustaining rapid economic growth. In 1995, the gross domestic saving rate in transition economies was 18% of GDP (EBRD, 1996), lower than the average world saving rate (23% of GDP), and much lower than in the case of the rapidly growing East Asian economies (35% of GDP). Promoting domestic saving in transition countries calls for slimmer government. On the one hand, lower budgetary spending would improve the balance of the budget and reduce government dissaving (or increase its savings). On the other hand, and this is of much greater importance, curtailing government spending would stimulate household savings, which play a dominant role in wealth accumulation in a market economy. In centrally-planned economies, household savings were very- low because of the low incentives to save. Since social security benefits were provided by the government, individuals perceived no need to save for retirement or for a 'rainy day'. Shifting the burden of social security from the government to the private sector would increase incentives for private savings. At the same time, this would have a positive impact on financial markets, stimulating the development of financial intermediaries (such as pension funds) and saving instruments.

These arguments make the measures to reduce the scope of fiscal redistribution in transition economies even more necessary and urgent.

4.2   Structural Analysis of the Expenditure Side

Between 1989 and 1995 the patterns of government expenditure changed drastically in transition economies (see Table 4.3).

Successful pro-market transformation of the economy requires, among other things, price liberalization and the reduction of price distortions. Typically, there is a strong connection between price liberalization and the decline in government spending on subsidies. When prices are allowed to reach market-determined levels which cover the producers' costs, subsidies become unnecessary. Thus, progress with price liberalization is reflected in a decrease in subsidies.

The most distinctive feature of changes in budgetary expenditures among Central European transition countries is the sharp drop in subsidies. Between 1989 and 1995, producer and consumer subsidies declined by 8.8% of GDP in Poland, by 8.5% of GDP in Hungary and by 17% of GDP in the Czech and Slovak Republics. The situation was different in Slovenia, since budgeted subsidies constituted a rather modest part of GDP (some 4%) in the former

Table 4.3   General government expenditures in Central European countries. In percent of GDP

	1989	1990	1991	1992	1993	1994	1995	Change 1989–95[c]
Poland								
Total expenditures	**39.9**	**43.6**	**48.9**	**51.8**	**49.9**	**50.5**	**49.8**	**+9.9**
Current expenditures	**36.4**	**39.7**	**45.7**	**48.4**	**46.7**	**47.4**	**47.3**	**+10.9**
• Goods and services	2.5	4.8	7.8	6.2	4.4	3.3	6.4	+3.9
• Wages and salaries	4.2	4.4	6.2	8.1	7.9	9.9	8.5	+4.3
• Interest payments	0.0	0.4	1.5	3.1	3.8	4.4	5.3	+5.3
• Subsidies	10.6	7.7	5.1	3.3	3.9	4.1	1.8	−8.8
• Transfers	10.4	18.9	20.7	19.9	20.6	21.6	21.0	+10.6
• Other current expenditures	2.8	3.5	4.4	7.7	6.1	4.2	4.3	+1.5
Capital expenditures	**3.4**	**3.9**	**3.2**	**3.4**	**3.3**	**3.1**	**2.5**	**−0.9**
Hungary								
Total expenditures	**60.5**	**57.2**	**54.0**	**60.6**	**61.6**	**62.1**	**55.3**	**−5.2**
Current expenditures	**53.9**	**52.5**	**48.2**	**52.9**	**55.1**	**55.5**	**49.9**	**−4.0**
• Goods and services	12.1	11.1	8.6	9.0	15.0	11.1	11.0	−1.1
• Wages and salaries	8.2	7.6	8.4	8.5	8.6	9.4	7.7	−0.5
• Interest payments	2.4	3.0	3.2	5.9	4.7	8.4	8.9	+6.5
• Subsidies	12.0	9.5	7.4	5.5	4.3	4.5	3.5	−8.5
• Transfers	19.2	21.3	20.6	24.0	22.5	22.2	18.8	−0.4
• Other current expenditures	0.0	0.0	0.0	0.0	0.0	0.0	0.0	0.0
Capital expenditures	**6.5**	**4.6**	**5.8**	**7.7**	**6.5**	**6.6**	**5.3**	**−1.2**
Czech Republic[a]								
Total expenditures	*58.9*	*49.5*	*52.2*	47.8	50.1	50.7	49.8	+2.0
Current expenditures	*53.5*	*45.0*	*51.2*	39.3	43.3	43.6	42.2	+2.9
• Goods and services	*11.7*	*11.4*	*14.1*	12.7	14.0	13.9	13.5	+0.8
• Wages and salaries	*2.6*	*2.4*	*4.3*	3.5	4.0	4.7	4.7	+1.2
• Interest payments	–	*0.2*	*0.5*	1.0	1.6	1.4	1.3	+0.3
• Subsidies	*22.0*	*13.4*	*9.0*	4.9	4.1	3.6	3.4	−1.5
• Transfers	*17.2*	*17.6*	*23.3*	17.2	19.5	20.1	19.4	+2.2
• Other current expenditures	–	–	–	0.0	0.0	0.0	0.0	⁄0.0
Capital expenditures	*7.5*	*6.7*	*5.3*	8.5	6.8	7.1	7.7	−0.8
Slovak Republic[a]								
Total expenditures	*58.9*	*49.5*	*52.2*	58.0	51.2	47.7	47.3	−10.7
Current expenditures	*53.5*	*45.0*	*51.2*	50.5	45.5	43.2	42.3	−8.2
• Goods and services	*11.7*	*11.4*	*14.1*	17.9	12.9	10.6	11.2	−6.7
• Wages and salaries	*2.6*	*2.4*	*4.3*	4.6	4.3	3.8	3.6	−1.0
• Interest payments	–	*0.2*	*0.5*	1.1	3.2	3.9	2.2	+1.1
• Subsidies	*22.0*	*13.4*	*9.0*	5.2	5.1	4.9	4.8	−0.4
• Transfers	*17.2*	*17.6*	*23.3*	21.7	20.1	20.0	20.5	+1.2
• Other current expenditures	–	–	–	0.0	0.0	0.0	0.0	0.0
Capital expenditures	*7.5*	*6.7*	*5.3*	7.5	5.7	4.5	5.0	−2.5
Slovenia[b]								
Total expenditures	**40.6**	**–**	**41.1**	**46.2**	**46.8**	**47.5**	**46.2**	**+5.1**
Current expenditures	**–**	**–**	**38.1**	**43.7**	**44.5**	**44.5**	**43.2**	**+5.1**
• Goods and services	12.1	–	–	1.5	1.3	1.5	1.5	–
• Wages and salaries		–	–	7.2	7.3	6.6	6.4	–
• Interest payments		–	0.3	0.5	1.3	1.5	1.5	+1.2
• Subsidies		–	5.2	5.3	4.2	3.8	3.7	−1.5
• Transfers		–	27.0	27.8	28.7	29.4	28.6	+1.6
• Other current expenditures		–	0.0	1.5	1.7	1.7	1.6	+1.6
Capital expenditures	**0.5**	**–**	**3.0**	**2.5**	**2.3**	**3.1**	**3.0**	**0.0**

[a] Data for 1989, 1990, 1991 refer to Czechoslovakia.
[b] Data for 1989, 1990 refer to Yugoslavia.
[c] For the Czech and Slovak Republics, change 1992–5; for Slovenia, change 1991–5.

Sources: MultiQuery Database: A Tool for Cross-Country Comparisons. Europe and Central Asia Region. The World Bank, Spring 1996. Data for Czechoslovakia and Yugoslavia: *Government Finance Statistics.* IMF, 1994.

Yugoslavia (Barbone and Polackova, 1996, p. 7). Consequently, reported budgetary costs of enterprise subsidies have almost disappeared in transition countries. In 1995, the budgetary subsidy to GDP ratio varied from 1.8% in Poland to 4.8% in the Slovak Republic.

It must be noted, however, that focusing only on reported budgetary subsidies in the assessment of the scope of government intervention in the economy, and from the viewpoint of the introduction of hard budget constraints to enterprises, can be misleading. It is a common feature of transition economies that the sharp reduction in direct producer subsidies had been accompanied by increases in tax arrears, as well as by increases in non-performing loans in the banking sector (Schaffer, 1995; Orlowski, 1996). In many post-communist economies there have also been large quasi-fiscal subsidies, mainly in the form of directed credit from or via the central bank, addressed to specific sectors (e.g., agriculture), or in the form of negative real interest rates; these quasi-fiscal subsidies sometimes even exceed officially recorded fiscal subsidies (see Dąbrowski, 1996). This phenomenon, however, widely experienced in countries of the former Soviet Union (FSU) and in Romania, was of rather marginal importance in CEE countries during the period under analysis.

Cuts in subsidies for products have often been transmitted into increased expenditure on transfers. Therefore, cuts in subsidies alone can not be perceived as evidence of sounder public finances and as a measure of success in re-introducing market rules. On the one hand, cuts in subsidies have not alleviated pressures on budget deficit (tax arrears—revenue losses, and increased transfers—see section 4.3 of this Chapter); on the other hand, they have not fully eliminated soft budget constraints to enterprises. Whereas, the former phenomenon is connected to fiscal adjustment itself, the latter means the postponement in necessary enterprise restructuring, the crucial step in pro-market transformation. It is worth noting that this concerns primarily large state-owned enterprises. In the case of Poland, for example, over a third of arrears on social security contributions at the end of 1995 originated with coal mines.

The most expensive burden on general government expenditure in transition economies is the maintenance of a social safety net system, with pensions as its most costly component. In 1995, current transfers absorbed some 20% of GDP, with levels varying from 18.8% of GDP in Hungary to 28.6% of GDP in Slovenia. Between 1989 and 1995, the share of transfers in GDP increased in all countries, except for Hungary.

Transition countries inherited from the socialist system an extensive social welfare system, generally comprising a pay-as-you-go (unfunded) state pension scheme, sick pay, generous maternity benefits and family allowances, retraining/labour funds, as well as specific welfare schemes. The social benefits paid were not related to the social security contributions, and the pension system was unfunded; general budget revenues provided the major source of financing the entire social security system. At the beginning of the transition process, the former centrally-planned economies were faced with the necessity of replacing this inefficient system with social safety net structures, suited to the requirement of a market economy. The need for implementation of cost-effective social safety nets was reinforced by the expected social costs of transformation, exerting pressure on growth in government expenditures in the form of unemployment benefits and various forms of social assistance.

The high share of current transfers in GDP, in view of the favourable output performance in 1994–5, is clear evidence that comprehensive, fundamental reforms of social security and welfare systems are not completed and still remain a major challenge in post-socialist countries.

The high level of pension benefits is one of the most important reasons for the expensive social security systems in transition economies. This is the outcome of both unfavourable demographic trends, and changes in the pensions systems which have taken place during a pro-market transformation. The high share of old-age and disability pensioners is partly the result of early retirements schemes and lax eligibility criteria, introduced as a surrogate for outright lay-offs. Additionally, in most Central European countries, statutory regulations on the indexation of pension benefits were introduced. Between 1989 and 1994, the replacement ratio (the ratio of average pension benefit to average wage) decreased by more than six percentage points in the Czech Republic, Slovakia, and Hungary, and have remained fairly stable in Slovenia. Different processes have taken place in Poland, where the replacement ratio increased during transition period by as much as 20 percentage points. In 1994, the ratio of average gross pension to average wage amounted to 73% in Poland and Slovenia, 57% in Hungary, 44% in the Czech Republic and 42% in the Slovak Republic (Golinowska, 1996, pp. 20–2). It seems obvious that pensions recipients in Poland and Slovenia obtain excessively generous compensation from the government. Such a situation reflects an unfair tendency in income redistribution to the advantage of pensioners.

The budgetary burden of pensions in these five CEE economies ranged in 1995 from 9.1% of GDP in the Czech Republic to 14.6% of GDP in Poland. These ratios are high by international standards—the average for OECD countries was 9.2% of GDP, while the averages for countries of comparable per capita income in Latin America and East Asia amounted to 2.0% and 1.9% of GDP, respectively (EBRD, 1996, p. 95). High levels of government pension spending are correlated with the low levels of private savings and private ownership of capital in transition economies, as discussed earlier.

Despite numerous statements on the inescapable and urgent need of real and serious reforms of the pension systems, the progress in this area has been poor. A general, broad consensus among social partners about the necessity of fundamental changes has not been translated into real steps towards structures compatible with a market economy.

The larger the privileges pensions recipients currently enjoy, the more difficult is the introduction of the required measures. Political instability creates additional obstacles to real pension system reforms, as pensioners constitute a considerable portion of the electorate. Both factors are unfavourable in Poland, where the current pension system does not really differ from the pre-transition one. It is still state-run, single-tier and unfunded.

The situation is similar in other transition countries. Rather cautious steps towards the multi-pillar structure of pension systems, with a more explicit link between individual contributions and pensions, were taken in the Czech Republic in 1994, and in Hungary in 1993. The supplementary pension schemes in the Czech Republic are largely connected with state budget subsidies (Stepanek et al., 1995). In Hungary, the role of pension fund system is negligible (Golinowska, 1996, p. 22). Therefore, although the progress in transition towards a sustainable public finance system in post-socialist countries is dependent on the comprehensive reforms of pension system, such reforms are still ahead.

The second burden on general expenditures in some transition countries is the coverage of unemployment benefits, together with the financing of various active labour market policy (ALMP) schemes. Unemployment insurance schemes, with benefits provided for a limited duration, have been introduced as part of the transformation process; the expected serious imbalance in the labour market called for the need to protect and support the affected workers until the time when systemic changes began to take effect. Legal regulations on unemployment were adopted in Hungary in 1988, in Poland in 1989, and in Czechoslovakia in 1991. During the course of transition, these regulations were amended frequently (see Golinowska, 1996, pp. 13–17), reflecting ongoing changes in the labour market. In Poland, where the unemployment insurance schemes initially introduced were extremely generous (unlimited duration of unemployment benefits, which were linked with individual's last earnings), the eligibility rules were tightened, benefits were limited to one year and were de-linked from past earnings. In other transition countries, eligibility criteria introduced in the first phase of transition were relatively tight, and the size of allowances rather modest.

Despite a favourable output performance in 1994 and 1995, unemployment remains high in Poland, with registered jobless amounting to 14.9% of the labour force in 1995, in Slovenia (13.5%), and in the Slovak Republic (13.1%). The high level of unemployment in Hungary (10.6%) can be attributed to the slower pace of economic recovery. The Czech Republic has avoided serious problems of rising registered unemployment—within the period from 1989 to 1995 its highest rate, recorded in 1991, amounted to 4.1%.

The share of expenditures on labour market schemes (unemployment benefits and the expenditures on ALMP schemes) in GDP is the lowest in the

Czech Republic (less than 0.5% in 1993) and the highest in Hungary (3%); these ratios are comparable to those seen in EU countries.

Special attention must be paid to public health care. The ratio of government expenditures on public health care to GDP have either increased (in the Czech Republic) or remained stable during the transition period. It must be stressed, that these services are still financed primarily from the government budget—the role of the private sector is marginal. To raise the quality of medical services, overall reforms in this area are needed. Some steps towards more effective health-care systems have been undertaken in Hungary and in the Czech and Slovak Republics. The general idea of the reforms being introduced was to separate health insurance funds from the state budget or social insurance fund. This would permit the creation of a system partially of an insurance character, financed from contributions paid by employers and employees. Although such funds were set up, they neither markedly solved the financial problems of health care institutions nor increased the low effectiveness of public health care (Uldrichova, 1996; Gyulavari and Nemenyi, 1996). In practice, the existing financial problems of the health-care sector led to the introduction of various charges and fees for patients, sometimes of informal character.

Transition economies experience a growing burden of debt interest payments in government expenditure. Between 1989 and 1995, the share of interest payments in GDP reached 8.9% in Hungary and 5.3% in Poland. At the beginning of the transition process these two countries were highly burdened with external debt, while the domestic debt played virtually no role in their total indebtedness. In the course of transition, the share of domestic debt has been more and more important for all the analysed countries. Because of the strong dynamics of the stock of domestic debt, the share of fixed costs connected with debt service in government expenditure has increased. Considering current and future borrowing needs of the public sector, this process is likely to continue.

In sum, government expenditure in transition countries is strongly dominated by current transfers, which still retain many features from the centrally-planned economy era. Changing unfavourable spending patterns and diminishing the role of the state are obviously conditioned by a fundamental reform of social security and welfare system, aiming at the re-directing of social demand in these areas from the government to the private sector.

4.3 Structural Analysis of the Revenue Side

Successful economic transformation requires a fundamental reform of the revenue side of the budget. Within the inherited fiscal system, budget revenues were heavily dependent on levies paid by state-owned enterprises and on turnover tax; taxes paid by households constituted only a marginal fraction of budget revenues. There were three main reasons for urgent changes in the tax system (Vaskova, 1996):

- the need to establish a system of general parametric profit taxation that would eliminate 'soft budget constraints' and support incentive-driven forces in the economy;
- the necessity of achieving universal and equal tax treatment of different sectors, commodities, and forms of ownership to ensure that resource allocation would be driven by undistorted market forces;
- adequate adjustment of individual income taxation in line with distributional objectives and institutional changes.

The tax reforms introduced in transition countries have followed West European revenue patterns. The previous turnover tax was replaced by consumption taxes—value-added tax (VAT) and specific excises. A personal income tax (PIT) was implemented to replace the previous range of taxes on income. VAT and PIT, together with corporate income tax and the payroll-based social security contributions, are the main channels of fiscal revenues.

VAT and PIT were first introduced in Hungary, in 1988. In the countries of former Czechoslovakia tax reform was carried out in 1993; in Poland, PIT was implemented in 1992 and VAT in July 1993.

The main goal of implementing VAT was to extend the indirect tax base to services and imports and to enhance its neutrality, by reducing the range of rates in comparison with the previous system. VAT was expected to reduce tax evasion as well.

The tax system reform has taken place during the overall macroeconomic adjustment process, under persisting inflationary pressures and with growing government expenditures, calling for sufficient fiscal capacity. Conflicting policy goals and targets have profoundly affected the development of tax structures; the main driving force of changes being implemented, within the new system, has been budgetary pressures.

The Hungarian VAT policy experience can serve as an example of difficulties in meeting different policy objectives in transition economies. In 1988, the standard VAT rate of 25% was accompanied by the preferential rate of 15%, applied to most services. To reduce the social costs and inflationary pressures, following the implementation of VAT, the zero rate was in force for most of the food products, fuels, pharmaceuticals, and public transport. Medical care, sports, culture, education, financial services, and public administration were VAT-exempted. In 1993, the government launched a large scale revision which lowered the reduced rate to 6% (from August 1993, 10%). This rate covered a group of products and services, previously taxed at zero rate (e.g., food, public transport). The zero rate remained only for

Table 4.4   General government revenues in Central European countries. In percent of GDP

	1989	1990	1991	1992	1993	1994	1995	Change 1989–95[c]
Poland								
Total revenues	**33.8**	**47.3**	**42.3**	**45.1**	**47.6**	**48.3**	**47.2**	**+13.4**
Current revenues	**33.8**	**47.0**	**42.1**	**44.7**	**46.8**	**47.2**	**46.1**	**+12.3**
Tax revenues	**30.3**	**41.6**	**35.6**	**38.1**	**40.7**	**40.7**	**40.4**	**+10.1**
• Corporate income tax	7.9	15.2	6.9	4.6	4.2	3.4	3.1	–4.8
• Personal income tax	4.2	4.8	5.8	8.9	9.7	9.9	9.7	+5.5
• VAT or sales tax	7.2	6.7	7.7	9.0	11.4	12.8	12.9	+5.7
• Trade taxes	0.0	0.7	2.1	2.3	2.8	2.3	2.0	+2.0
• Other taxes	2.3	2.9	2.8	2.0	1.6	1.5	1.5	–0.8
• Social sec. contribution	8.7	11.4	10.5	11.4	11.0	10.8	11.1	+2.4
Non-tax revenues	**3.5**	**5.4**	**6.4**	**6.6**	**6.1**	**6.5**	**5.7**	**+2.2**
Capital revenues	**0.0**	**0.3**	**0.2**	**0.4**	**0.8**	**1.1**	**1.1**	**+1.1**
Hungary								
Total revenues	**59.2**	**57.6**	**51.9**	**55.2**	**54.9**	**54.6**	**51.3**	**–7.9**
Current revenues	**59.2**	**54.8**	**51.9**	**54.4**	**54.6**	**53.8**	**47.9**	**–11.3**
Tax revenues	**49.9**	**44.7**	**42.1**	**40.8**	**41.7**	**38.2**	**37.0**	**–12.9**
• Corporate income tax	8.1	7.5	5.3	2.5	2.0	2.0	1.1	–7.0
• Personal income tax	5.5	6.1	6.9	7.5	8.0	7.1	6.8	+1.3
• VAT or sales tax	7.8	7.0	6.0	6.0	8.1	7.7	7.6	–0.3
• Trade taxes	5.3	5.4	3.0	3.4	3.5	3.4	4.4	–0.9
• Other taxes	9.0	5.0	7.8	7.9	6.6	5.5	5.3	–3.7
• Social sec. contribution	14.2	13.7	13.0	13.5	13.4	12.5	11.8	–2.4
Non-tax revenues	**9.3**	**10.0**	**9.8**	**13.6**	**12.9**	**15.6**	**10.9**	**+1.6**
Capital revenues	**0.0**	**2.9**	**0.0**	**0.8**	**0.3**	**0.8**	**3.4**	**+3.4**
Czech Republic[a]								
Total revenues	*56.8*	*49.3*	*50.0*	**48.2**	**51.4**	**51.2**	**50.4**	**+2.2**
Current revenues	–	–	–	**48.2**	**50.6**	**49.4**	**49.2**	**+1.0**
Tax revenues	–	–	–	**41.6**	**45.4**	**44.6**	**45.1**	**+3.5**
• Corporate income tax	*10.3*	*11.5*	*13.3*	10.8	7.8	6.2	5.0	–5.8
• Personal income tax	*0.0*	*0.0*	*5.8*	7.0	3.3	5.3	5.7	–1.3
• VAT or sales tax	*17.7*	*18.2*	*12.6*	0.0	7.7	8.3	8.1	+8.1
• Trade taxes	*1.8*	*3.2*	*1.2*	1.6	1.7	1.7	1.5	–0.1
• Other taxes	*0.5*	*0.3*	–	11.9	8.4	5.9	6.4	–5.5
• Social sec. contribution	–	–	–	10.3	16.6	17.3	18.5	+8.2
Non-tax revenues	–	–	–	**6.6**	**5.2**	**4.9**	**4.1**	**–2.5**
Capital revenues	–	–	–	**0.0**	**0.8**	**1.8**	**1.2**	**+1.2**
Slovak Republic[a]								
Total revenues	*56.8*	*49.3*	*50.0*	**46.1**	**44.2**	**46.4**	**47.9**	**+1.8**
Current revenues	–	–	–	**46.1**	**44.2**	**46.4**	**47.9**	**+1.8**
Tax revenues	–	–	–	**39.4**	**36.4**	**38.8**	**39.4**	**0.0**
• Corporate income tax	*10.3*	*11.5*	*13.3*	9.4	6.0	7.2	6.6	–2.8
• Personal income tax	*0.0*	*0.0*	*5.8*	7.0	3.9	4.1	4.7	–2.3
• VAT or sales tax	*17.7*	*18.2*	*12.6*	0.0	7.4	8.4	11.5	+11.5
• Trade taxes	*1.8*	*3.2*	*1.2*	1.6	1.2	1.6	2.1	+0.5
• Other taxes	*0.5*	*0.3*	–	12.4	6.2	5.7	3.2	–9.2
• Social sec. contribution	–	–	–	9.1	11.6	11.7	11.4	+2.3
Non-tax revenues	–	–	–	**6.7**	**7.8**	**7.6**	**8.4**	**+1.8**
Capital revenues	–	–	–	**0.0**	**0.0**	**0.0**	**0.0**	**0.0**
Slovenia[b]								
Total revenues	*42.7*	–	**43.7**	**46.4**	**47.1**	**47.3**	**45.9**	**+2.2**
Current revenues	–	–	**43.7**	**46.4**	**47.1**	**47.3**	**45.9**	**+2.2**
Tax revenues	–	–	**40.7**	**42.2**	**43.0**	**44.0**	**43.9**	**+3.2**
• Corporate income tax	–	–	0.6	0.6	0.5	0.8	0.6	0.0
• Personal income tax	–	–	6.7	6.9	6.8	7.5	6.9	+0.3
• VAT or sales tax	*28.3*	–	10.2	10.8	11.1	12.8	13.5	+3.4
• Trade taxes	*13.3*	–	3.6	3.2	3.6	3.6	3.7	+0.1
• Other taxes	–	–	0.0	0.0	0.0	0.0	0.0	0.0
• Social sec. contribution	–	–	19.6	20.8	21.0	19.3	19.1	–0.5
Non-tax revenues	–	–	**3.0**	**4.2**	**4.1**	**3.3**	**2.0**	**–1.1**
Capital revenues	–	–	**0.0**	**0.0**	**0.0**	**0.0**	**0.0**	**0.0**

[a] Data for 1989, 1990, 1991 refer to Czechoslovakia.
[b] Data for 1989, 1990 refer to Yugoslavia.
[c] For the Czech and Slovak Republics, change 1992–5; for Slovenia, change 1991–5.

Sources: MultiQuery Database: A Tool for Cross-Country Comparisons. Europe and Central Asia Region. The World Bank, Spring 1996. Data for Czechoslovakia and Yugoslavia: *Government Finance Statistics.* IMF, 1994.

Table 4.5   Tax rates in Central European and European Union countries

	VAT[a]		Social security contributions[b]		Corporate income tax[c, d]
	Reduced	Standard	Employees	Employers	
Poland	7	22.0	0	48.0	40.0
Hungary	12	25.0	11.0	47.0	18.0
Czech Republic	5	22.0	13.25	35.25	39.0
Slovak Republic	6	25.0	12.0	38.0	40.0
Belgium	1, 6, 12	21.0	13.1	34.2	39.0
Denmark	–	25.0	2.6	0	34.0
France	2.1, 5.5	20.6	18.4	n.a.	33.3
Germany	7	15.0	18.3	18.3	45/30
Greece	4, 8	18.0	15.8	27.4	40.0
Ireland	2.5, 12.5	21.0	8.8	12.2	40.0
Italy	4, 9, 13	19.0	10.0	46.0	52.2
Luxembourg	3, 6, 12	15.0	12.5	14.9	39.4
Netherlands	6	15.5	29.3	7.2	35.0
Portugal	5	16.0	11.0	24.5	39.6
Spain	3, 6	15.0	6.1	31.6	35.0
United Kingdom	0	17.5	7.6	10.4	33.0

[a] VAT rates for 1995.
[b] For Central European countries, data for 1995; for EU countries, data from 1990–3.
[c] For Central European countries, data for 1996; for EU countries, for 1994.
[d] Where two rates are given, the latter is the rate on retained profits.

Source: Vaskova (1996).

household energy and medicines. From January 1995 the preferential rate was increased to 12%. Some products and services previously classified in this category were reclassified and taxed at the standard rate.

From 1988 to 1992 the share of VAT revenues in Hungarian GDP decreased (see Table 4.4). The proportion of zero rate goods and services within a household's purchases reached the level of 44% in 1991 (Gyulavari and Nemenyi, 1996, p. 64). The revision of VAT rates in 1993 led to the increase of VAT to GDP ratio in 1993, but in 1994 and 1995 this share decreased again.

The lesson from the Hungarian case is straightforward. First, although the introduction of VAT leads to a (once-only) price increase, the whole tax adjustment process should be carried out relatively quickly. A broad application of the zero and reduced rates erodes the principle of VAT neutrality and distorts consumer and producer decisions. Second, high tax rates do not bring about high budgetary revenues; in fact, they tend to diminish the tax collection capacity. In Hungary, the application and extension of high VAT rates led to a considerable tax evasion; according to some researchers (Gyulavari and Nemenyi, 1996, p. 64), VAT avoidance seems to be the rule rather than the exception in some sectors of the Hungarian economy.

The situation in Poland, the Czech Republic and Slovakia is similar. Commodities originally taxed at the zero turnover tax rate are still taxed at the reduced rate. At the same time, budgetary needs (pressures on expenditures) are the main cause of maintaining high—in comparison with EU countries—standard rates of VAT (see Table 4.5).

The pattern of PIT among transition countries differs in details concerning deductions and exemptions. In general, PIT has a progressive structure of marginal rates. In 1996 these rates ranged from 0% to 45% in Poland, from 0% to 48% in Hungary, from 15% to 40% in the Czech Republic and from 15% to 42% in the Slovak Republic.

All transition countries have implemented mandatory, payroll-based social security contributions, which cover pension, sickness, unemployment, and health insurance in the Czech and Slovak Republics; pension, sickness, and unemployment insurance in Hungary, and pension and unemployment insurance in Poland. The social security rates are given in Table 4.5.

Social security contributions paid by employers increase considerably the cost of labour. This strengthens the incentive for tax evasion and has negative consequences for employment (lower formal hirings). The rates applied in Poland and Hungary are well above the rates of EU countries, except for Italy, where it amounts to 46%.

Corporate income tax rates differ among four CEE countries, varying in 1996 from 18% for retained profits and 23% for distributed profits in Hungary, 39% in the Czech Republic, to 40% in Poland and the Slovak Republic. In all countries, except for Poland, the rates were reduced between 1993 and 1996.

As a result of the reforms of the tax system, the patterns of government revenues changed considerably between 1989 and 1995 (see Table 4.4). The significance of corporate income tax decreased in each of the analysed transition countries, but by far the greatest in Hungary; the share of individual income tax in GDP increased. VAT revenues, as measured by the ratio to GDP, vary from 7.6% in Hungary to 13.5% in Slovenia. Social security contributions are the main revenue source in Slovenia, in the Czech Republic and in Hungary.

Due to the expansion of government expenditure, maintaining fiscal revenues has been a major challenge in all countries in transition. Despite the reforms within the tax system, and a favourable output performance in 1994–5, government revenues have not significantly increased. Weak tax collection is undoubtedly connected with high tax rates, leading to tax arrears and numerous methods of tax evasion. These high tax rates are accompanied, however, by widespread exemptions and deductions. In addition, poor revenue performance can be attributed to weak tax administration.

Tax collection could be improved by broadening the tax base and lowering marginal tax rates, together with better tax administration. But beyond paying attention to the revenue side of the budget, the fundamental reforms of the expenditure side are required to develop a sound public finance situation in the transition countries.

Notes

1. This chapter was written with the assistance of Ryszard Petru who prepared most of the statistical information. The author represents CASE (Center for Social and Economic Research), a private international research and policy advising institution in Warsaw, specializing in problems of the post-communist transition process. The author used extensively in this paper the results and conclusions of an earlier research project on 'The Fiscal Crisis in Central and Eastern Europe under Transition' carried out by CASE during the period January 1994–May 1996 and financed by the Ford Foundation. The chapter draws in particular on work done by Andrzej S. Bratkowski, Jaroslaw Bauc, Pavel Stepanek, Drahomira Vaskova, Vera Kamenickova, Vera Uldrichova, Milena Horcicova, Stefan Adamec, Antal Gyulavari, Judit Nemenyi, Lucjan T. Orlowski, Malgorzata Antczak, Marcin Luczynski, Krzysztof Polomski, Alain de Crombrugghe, Barbara Fakin, Luca Barbone, Hana Polackova, Jeffrey Sachs, and Andrew Warner. Of course, the author of this chapter takes exclusive responsibility for its content, quality, and conclusions.
2. It must be noted, however, that dealing with transition economies data needs special attention because of numerous methodological issues. For example, the Hungarian National Accounts introduced the 1993 SNA recommendation in 1993 and recalculated the GDP data from 1991; the new level of GDP became higher. Consequently, the share of revenues and expenditures in GDP dropped automatically by almost 4% in 1991. For further details on Hungarian fiscal information system see Gyulavari and Nemenyi (1996), vol. II, pp. 40–2.
3. A lot of research suggests a negative correlation between the level of fiscal redistribution and the rate of economic growth. Allowing for the level of GDP per capita, it has been estimated that an additional 10 percentage points in the government expenditures GDP ratio is associated with a 1 percentage point lower growth rate. See Balcerowicz and Gelb (1995), p. 30, quoting from Easterly and Rebelo (1993), and section 5.2 of this report.

5

Fiscal Policy: a Long-Term View

Fabrizio Coricelli

The long-term implications of current fiscal trends can be assessed in connection with two main issues. The first is the sustainability from a macroeconomic point of view of current budget deficits. This involves assessing the implication of current budget deficits for the dynamics of public debt, and the consistency of such dynamics with the overall macroeconomic objectives of the government, especially in terms of inflation.

The second issue relates to the implications of the size of the government and of budget deficits for future economic growth. Typically, budget deficits have an impact on growth through their effect on inflation and on the financing of private sector activity ('crowding-out'). In contrast, the size of the government (measured as the ratio of public expenditure to GDP) may affect growth through the effects of taxation, public investments and public transfers on private savings. Different types of expenditures tend to have different effects on growth. Finally, the size of the government is linked to the redistributive role of public expenditures and taxes.[1]

5.1   Sustainability of Fiscal Policy

When the public sector runs a budget deficit in a given year, it faces three options in subsequent years. One is to maintain a deficit and finance it through money creation. The second is to maintain the deficit and finance it through public debt. The third is to eliminate the deficit by balancing expenditures and revenues. The first option, money financing, implies that the deficit is financed through the seignorage from money creation. Seignorage is defined as the amount of real resources a government can extract from the public by printing money. Technically, it is the rate of change of the money stock (base money) divided by the price level. To have a meaningful quantitative assessment of seignorage, such an amount is usually measured in terms of GDP. The change in base money in real terms, and measured in terms of real GDP, is composed of three elements. One is the change in real base money that is desired by the public. The second is the product of inflation and real base money (the so-called inflation tax). From the point of view of the public, this is the reduction of the real value of money due to inflation. Finally, as we measure stocks in terms of GDP, there is the product of the real growth of output and the initial stock of real base money. Thus, a higher rate of growth of output implies that the government can extract more seignorage (in terms of GDP) for a given rate of inflation.

The amount of seignorage is constrained by the demand for money of the public. Indeed, a higher rate of inflation generates a larger inflation tax; however, demand for money declines with higher inflation. Thus, the base for the inflation tax declines. After a certain rate of inflation, seignorage may in fact fall with higher inflation. Demand for money, therefore, sets limits to the size of the deficit that can be financed through seignorage. Given the parameters of the demand for money function and institutional arrangements concerning reserve requirements, one can compute the level of seignorage associated with each level of inflation (and rate of growth of the economy). In market economies—and in normal times—seignorage tends to be relatively small, on the order of 1–1.5% of GDP. Reluctance to tolerate high inflation rates leads most countries to rely on debt financing of deficits (the second option stressed above).

When the government accumulates debt, the sustainability of budget deficits can be judged in terms of the implied dynamics of public debt. If interest rates on public debt are higher than the rate of growth of the economy, debt as a ratio of GDP grows without bounds. The public is likely to react to such dynamics and would be reluctant to hold public debt. In this case, the government cannot keep financing the deficit and debt service by issuing new debt. Sooner or later it has to repay the old debt by running primary surpluses. In other words, when interest rates are higher than the rate of growth of the economy, the government faces an intertemporal budget constraint, which states that the present value of expenditure is equal to the present value of taxes. The practical implications of such a constraint for policy-makers are not easy to identify. In practice, governments tend to establish targets for debt-to-GDP ratios perceived as sustainable. Yet, should a government aim at stabilizing the debt ratio at 60% of GDP (the Maastricht requirement), or at 30% of GDP (the target assumed by New Zealand)? And over what time frame?

Setting targets on debt-to-GDP ratios permits a meaningful discussion of budgetary trends. Although a consistent analysis of sustainable deficits is not feasible, one can establish what is the financeable deficit consistent with debt-to-GDP ratios, inflation rates and rates of growth of the economy. Once such financeable deficit is computed, it can be compared with the actual deficit and the required adjustment to the primary deficit derived (the third option above).

Summing up, on a pragmatic level, it would be useful to assess fiscal adjustment in transition countries in the context of implied debt targets. Although there are measurement problems—from which even the calculation of traditional cash-flow or accrual budget balance is not immune—such an approach has important implications for economic policy.

As emphasized by Buiter (1997) and van Wijnbergen et al. (1991), among others, looking at fiscal sustainability would imply concentrating on the so-called operational, or real, deficit. This implies, first of all, that the relevant definition of the public sector consolidates the government and central bank accounts (see the Appendix). Second, the focus is shifted towards the absorption of real, rather than nominal, resources by the public sector. The accounting framework is similar to the one of an enterprise and relates the real deficit to the change in the net worth of the public sector as a whole.[2] As shown in the Appendix, the real or operational deficit can be derived, linking the real consolidated deficit to its sources of financing.

The consolidation of central bank and government accounts is particularly relevant to avoid hiding deficits in the central bank account. A case in point is when the central bank holds the external debt, as in Hungary for instance; this means external debt service is effected by the central bank, and therefore does not appear as a fiscal cost. Furthermore, measuring the change in stocks brings to the surface hidden subsidies, such as subsidized credit from the central bank via negative real interest rates. Indeed, negative real interest rates erode over time the real stock of central bank assets (refinancing credit or other firms of credit provided by the central bank to the economy).

As an illustration, Table 5.1 displays estimates of operational deficits and nominal deficits for some Central and East European (CEE) countries (Budina, 1997). The difference between the two budget indicators contained in Table 5.1 arises from two sources. First, the nominal budget deficit does not consolidate government and central bank accounts. Thus, differences arise due to different coverage of the two indicators. Second, there is a difference due to the fact that operational deficits exclude (i) the inflation component of interest rates on debt, and on central bank assets, (ii) the exchange rate component of interest rates on external debt. These effects differ sharply depending on the debt position of the countries. In Romania, for instance, domestic debt was small, while domestic assets of the central bank large, if compared to established market economies, as refinancing and directed credit by the central bank represented a significant share of domestic credit. Thus, a significant component of interest revenues for the central bank represented simply an inflationary component. Adjusting for this, real deficits appear larger than the nominal deficit. By contrast, in Bulgaria and Poland, government debt was

Table 5.1   Nominal government and operational (consolidated) deficit. In percent of GDP

	1992	1993	1994	1995
Bulgaria				
nominal deficit		10.9	5.5	5.69
operational deficit		2.92	−5.69	−1.55
Romania				
nominal deficit	2.32	0.84	2.28	
operational deficit	14.02	1.49	6.59	
Poland				
nominal deficit			2.2	2.6
operational deficit			2.6	3.8

Source: Budina (1997) and Chapter 4 of this Report.

very large, and, thus, the operational deficit tends to be smaller than the nominal one, as a significant proportion of interest payments represent only an inflation component.

In addition to the computation of operational deficits, the methodology summarized in the Appendix, linking the real deficit to its sources of financing, can be used to compute the required fiscal adjustment consistent with debt targets and inflation targets. It should be stressed that most variables in the key expression in the Appendix (equation 5) are endogenous (except for the foreign interest rate and foreign inflation). Nevertheless, the approach may provide a useful consistency framework for policy-makers. Indeed, if one takes the rate of growth of the economy as exogenous, demand for base money can be used to derive the rate of inflation consistent with a given target of debt/GDP ratio and given budget deficit, or time paths for deficit and debt.

Alternatively, one can fix the target rate of inflation and the total debt-to-GDP-ratio. Parameters of money demand would give the implied seignorage. Thus, one can compute the budget deficit consistent with government targets. Comparing this deficit with the actual real deficit, one can compute the required fiscal adjustment associated with different rates of inflation.[3]

Taking 1994 as a base year, Budina (1997) estimated that Romania needed a fiscal adjustment (as a ratio to GDP) of 6.33% at zero inflation, 4 % at a 62% inflation rate, and a minimum of 3.89% at a 110% inflation rate. Above this rate of inflation, revenue from the inflation tax would decline due to the dominant effect of shrinking demand for money. Taking 1995 as a base year, Budina (1997) finds that if Poland switches to market rates on its debt service (both domestic and foreign) the required fiscal adjustment would be 3.2% at zero inflation, and 0.97% at 29% inflation. Thus, inflation rates between 20% and 30% permit Poland to run a deficit which is 2% higher than the one that could be financed at zero inflation rate. The development of domestic bond market and increased international credibility—which reduces the cost of foreign borrowing—can allow Poland to gradually reduce the importance of the inflation tax as a source of deficit financing.

5.2   The Size of Governments, Budget Deficits and Growth

Empirical analysis on the effect of the size of government and budget deficits on growth is highly controversial. A number of cross-country studies (Barro, 1991; Levine and Renelt, 1992) have found that government expenditure has a negative impact on growth. Using the ratio of current expenditure to GDP as explanatory variable, the size of the negative effect is quite large. Fischer et al. (1996) have computed projected growth rates for some transition economies on the basis of the Barro and Levine and Renelt equations. In Table 5.2 we isolate the effect of government expenditure on projected growth rates.

The implied loss in output growth is staggering. If these equations were correct, a reduction of the size of current government expenditure (excluding transfers) in transition economies to the average levels of established market economies[4]—from about 18% of GDP to about 10%—would nearly double their growth rates. It should be noted, however, that transfers, and in particular social security expenditures, are not included in the variable used in the regressions. Sala-i-Martin (1996) has recently estimated a cross-country regression that suggests that social security expenditures affect positively the rate of growth of the economy[5]. Thus, different components of public expenditures have different effects on growth rates. The positive effect on growth of social security transfers is puzzling. Indeed, economic theory suggests that the prevailing pay-as-you-go (unfunded) systems have a negative effect on private savings and thus on investment and growth.

One possible explanation for such a puzzling effect is that more generous pension systems reduce the participation rates of older generations. People tend to retire earlier. The outcome is that the composition of the labour force shifts towards younger workers. Assume that production is characterized by innovations that require adaptation of workers through accumulation of usable human capital. Assume also that younger workers can more easily develop

Table 5.2   Selected Countries in Transition: Simulated Growth Rates (Barro, 1991)

Equation 1: Per capita growth=0.032–0.0075 initial per capita income +0.025 primary school enrolment +0.0305 secondary school enrolment –0.119 government consumption as a share of GDP

	Simulated Per Capita Growth Rates (Baseline)	Effect of Government Consumption	In Percent of Total Growth
Czech Republic	4.24	–3.38	–56.1
Hungary	5.24	–1.19	–22.7
Poland	4.59	–2.14	–46.7
Romania	5.16	–1.67	–32.3
Bulgaria	4.28	–2.02	–47.3
Russia	5.32	–2.02	–38.0
Transition countries (average 15 countries)	4.75	–2.14	–45.1

Source: Based on approach suggested by Fischer, Sahay and Vegh (1996).

such human capital. In such a context, there is an externality associated with the number of younger workers. The higher their proportion, the higher the productivity of the system. Under these assumptions, by inducing retirement of older workers, pension systems have a positive effect of productivity and thus, on growth (Sala-i-Martin, 1996).

The empirical relevance of such a reasoning is of course an open question. As noted, however, in Chapter 3 of this report (on restructuring), the experience of several transition economies has been precisely that of a surge in the number of retirees at the outset of reforms. Pensions have absorbed a large share of people out of state employment. The potential improvement in productivity associated to the changed composition of the labour force should be weighed against the pressure on budgetary expenditures. A crucial aspect that makes the results of Sala-i-Martin a possibly misleading predictor of future trends is that the demographic situation of many established market economies and of transition economies has changed significantly with respect to the 1970s and 1980s, namely, dependency ratios have sharply increased. With high dependency ratios it is likely that the possible productivity effects are overshadowed by the negative fiscal effects. Nevertheless, the productivity effects stressed by Sala-i-Martin (1996) are very relevant during the transition period.

Even more controversial than current expenditure is the impact of investment expenditure on output growth. In this respect, the literature points to a fundamental distinction between investment in infrastructure and investment of public enterprises. Investment in infrastructure tends to have a relevant positive effect on growth. In contrast, investment by public enterprises tends to have a negative effect on growth (Easterly and Rebelo, 1993).

In this area transition economies fare very poorly. Indeed, possibly with the exception of Hungary, public investment expenditure (excluding investment of state firms) as a ratio of GDP has fallen to extremely low levels, significantly lower than those in market economies. A positive development is given by the fact that investment of public enterprises is no longer financed by the budget.

Budget Deficits and Growth

Evidence from developing and developed countries tends to show the presence of a negative relation between budget deficit and output growth (Table 5.3). The channel that seems to emerge from the data is through a negative effect of budget deficits on private savings.[6]

One important channel of crowding-out in CEE countries works through bank financing of budget deficits, reducing available funds for financing enterprises (Calvo and Kumar, 1993). Crowding-out of credit has usually

Table 5.3 Developing Countries: Fiscal Deficits and Economic Performance[a]
Annual averages; in percent of GDP

	Small Fiscal Deficit			Moderate Fiscal Deficit			Large Fiscal Deficit		
	1975–82	1983–89	1990–95	1975–82	1983–89	1990–95	1975–82	1983–89	1990–95
Central government fiscal balance[b]	−0.2	−1.4	−1.2	−6.7	−6.0	−3.5	−5.5	−12.1	−6.0
Real GDP[c]	5.1	6.4	6.9	3.0	2.6	5.0	4.6	3.2	3.1
Consumer prices[d]	13.2	12.2	14.4	34.5	51.5	33.8	15.4	29.3	16.6
Consumer prices (median)	11.0	7.5	9.2	12.6	8.2	8.4	12.0	10.4	13.0
Current expenditure	13.4	14.9	14.9	18.9	17.6	17.5	22.0	27.3	21.9
Private saving	19.7	29.0	29.0	20.2	18.4	16.3	19.1	18.9	13.9
Private investment	16.0	19.9	19.9	10.0	12.6	15.6	14.9	12.4	14.9
Current account balance	−2.0	−0.1	−0.1	−2.1	−2.8	−3.3	1.6	−3.1	−3.6
Terms of trade	1.1	0.4	0.4	0.7	−1.0	−0.4	3.4	−0.4	−1.0
Real effective exchange rate	0.7	2.5	2.5	−0.8	−1.1	2.0	1.1	−2.5	−3.5
External debt	21.8	27.6	27.6	26.3	−46.8	48.9	27.3	47.4	52.2

[a] The classification of small, moderate and large fiscal deficit countries is based on the average deficit-to-GDP ratio for the period 1983–9.
[b] Including grant.
[c] Annual percentage change.
[d] Excluding Brazil.

Source: IMF, *World Economic Outlook*, October 1996.

taken place through the purchase of government bonds by commercial banks, shifting their assets towards safe government bonds and away from riskier enterprise loans.

Another channel explaining the negative impact of budget deficits on growth in transition economies works through inflation. Several studies illustrate the reasons why high inflation adversely affects output (see Bruno and Easterly, 1995). Inflation reduces financial savings and, thus, funds available for credit to the private sector.

It should be stressed, however, that the relation between output and inflation is likely to be highly non-linear (De Gregorio and Sturzenegger, 1994). Thus, very high inflation has a negative impact on output. In contrast, at moderate levels, inflation has no effect on growth, or, if any, it may have a positive effect, as predicted by the Phillips curve. The implication is that reducing high inflation has important benefits in terms of output and growth. Reducing moderate inflation, however, may be very costly for the real economy (Dornbusch and Fischer, 1992).

Debt Dynamics

Comparing the experience of the CEE countries with countries of the FSU, a clear difference can be noted in the rates of inflation and the size of the budget deficit (see World Bank, 1996). In contrast, and similarly to that found in studies on market economies, the short-term relation between budget deficits and inflation in CEE economies is weak and ambiguous. One possible reason is that measured budget deficits do not reflect the actual underlying inflationary pressure coming from the public sector as a whole (see section 5.1).

More generally, in CEE countries domestic debt and foreign financing played an increasingly important role. In this respect, country experiences have been heterogeneous. Indeed, the CEE countries began transition with significantly different volumes of inherited public debt, mainly foreign debt. Bulgaria, Hungary and Poland had accumulated large stocks of foreign debt during the pre-reform period, while the former Czechoslovakia and Romania had insignificant amounts of foreign debt at the end of the 1980s.

Bulgaria and Poland had serious difficulties in servicing their external debt, debt that was restructured after reforms in both countries (on the basis of the Paris Club agreement signed in 1991 in Poland, and of the London Club agreement reached in 1994 for Bulgaria). By contrast, Hungary remained current in its foreign debt service. Bulgaria and Poland, however, had not serviced their external debt before agreements on debt reduction. Thus, these agreements, while improving the solvency of the countries, initially implied a larger transfer abroad, as market rates were applied to the remaining stock of debt. This effect was particularly serious in Bulgaria.

Over time, among the highly indebted countries, only in Hungary did the ratio of total debt to GDP increase. In all countries there was a shift in the distribution of debt in favour of domestic versus foreign debt. This was due, partly, to financial sector restructuring, leading to recapitalization of banks, and to bond financing of deficits. It is unclear whether such a move was well-designed. Domestic debt increases the incentives for governments to wash away debts via step-inflation or devaluation. These incentives may be incorporated in the expectations of the public, making more complicated the reduction of inflation.

There is, thus, an important trade-off for policy-makers. The use of inflation tax, as long as inflation does not go above moderate levels, may be preferable to the increase of domestic debt. In general, it has been argued (Dornbusch and Fischer, 1992) that the costs of reducing rapidly moderate levels of inflation (say 20%) may be larger than the benefits. Especially in situations of substantial financial openness and financial instability, however, even moderate inflation may give rise to capital flight and pressure on the exchange rate.[7]

Most transition economies find themselves in the range of moderate inflation rates and policy-makers face the choice of how rapidly inflation should be reduced. Country experiences differ in this regard. In countries with higher debt ratios, inflation persisted at relatively high levels. The inflation tax remained important, even after the initial period of burst of inflation (Buiter, 1997). In addition to the lack of domestic bond markets, one reason for the reliance on the inflation tax might be that the costs of regular taxes is likely to be high, because of the inefficient structure of the tax system, dominated by highly distortionary taxes. Thus, although the medium-term goal remains the reduction of inflation to EU levels, such a reduction is likely to take place only gradually.[8]

An indication of excessive concern with the rapid decline of inflation in some of the most advanced countries in the last two years may come from the large inflows of foreign capital that characterized the Czech Republic, Hungary, Poland and Slovenia, and the difficulties these countries had in dealing with their monetary implications. Although there are several causes for the surge in capital inflows, they were also affected by a mix of fiscal and monetary policies biased towards excessive monetary tightening.

Sterilization of Capital Inflows

As transition moves on, the CEE countries begin to look more similar to market economies and to share several of the typical fiscal problems encountered especially in developing countries during post-stabilization periods.

With the first signs of success in stabilization and with the beginning of recovery in output, several CEE countries began to experience a sudden surge in inflow of foreign capital (Hungary, Poland and the Czech Republic). In fact, together with the restructuring of the banking sector, attempts to sterilize capital inflows have been the main source of increase of domestic debt in CEE economies.

Dealing with large capital inflows has proved to be extremely difficult for transition economies. Although capital inflows are needed from a long-term perspective of development—to finance the restructuring period and smooth out some of the temporary costs of transition—the sudden increase in capital inflows created serious difficulties for the management of monetary and fiscal policy.

Sterilization of capital inflows involved significant fiscal costs, as the central bank drained liquidity from the economy by selling interest-bearing bonds. Moreover, the cost of sterilization is magnified by the fact that sterilization itself, by raising interest rates, fosters additional inflows.[9]

Given the underdevelopment of securities markets, central bank bonds are placed at commercial banks. Holdings of safe government bonds reduce loanable funds of banks, crowding out loans to private firms. Increasing reserve requirements may be a better option from a fiscal point of view. Reserve requirements, however, are already at high levels in CEE economies, and their further increase would impose a high tax on financial intermediation.

To summarize, in the most advanced countries fiscal pressures and a build-up of domestic debt was affected by large capital inflows. The fiscal costs are not a necessary by-product of capital inflows, but they arise from the policy response to them. In countries with already relatively large stocks of public debt, sterilization policies may be very costly. On the other hand, in highly indebted economies, unsterilized capital flows may lead to a serious instability of the financial system. This problem seems to be particularly acute in

Hungary. In all countries, the decline of inflation rates toward Western European levels seems to be impaired by the large capital inflows. Considering, however, the overall transition problems of these economies it is unclear whether a rapid convergence towards Western European inflation rates is a reasonable or desirable target.

The adverse effects of an expansion of domestic debt, combined with large premia on interest rates remain a serious issue. An alternative to the inflation tax could be the use of index-linked debt instruments. These could avoid an increase of real interest rates, and, thus, debt service, along the path of declining inflation. Indeed, indexation of a part of government debt would reduce the incentives to inflate away the debt, and, thus, would reduce risk premia associated with the internalization of such government incentives by the public.[10]

Contingent Liabilities and Implicit Debt

In addition to official debt, fiscal pressure in the future is going to be decisively affected by the present build-up of implicit debt, which is not reported in official accounts. Two main sources of this implicit debt can be identified: the bad loans of banks, with effects even in the short run; and implicit pension liabilities, with major implications for long-term growth.

If the government de facto insures bank deposits, the negative net worth of banks that are saddled with assets of no value (bad loans), should be considered as public debt. These issues are particularly relevant in transition economies, where at the beginning of reform most of the economy was owned by the state.[11] This would imply that bank deposits should be considered public debt. In net terms, net debt would be equal to deposits net of performing loans, or, more simply, bad loans would be part of public debt. If credit, however, is mainly directed to state-owned enterprises, a proper measure of public debt would be given by deposits of households. For the state sector as a whole, loans, as well as enterprise deposits, net out. What is left is simply the government liability vis-à-vis the household sector, the only sector not belonging to the state sphere. To put it simply, in the initial stages of transition, the relevant measure of domestic debt might be broad money (net of enterprise deposits).[12]

Even if one follows the more conventional view that the public sector is composed of the central bank and the government sector, it is hardly disputable that bad loans at the commercial banks should be considered part of public debt. Adding bad loans to public debt would significantly modify the picture obtained when comparing official measures of public debt. One main change would be a much smaller difference between the debt/GDP ratios of the Czech Republic and those of Hungary and Poland.[13]

In 1995, the financial position of the banking system in the Czech Republic continued to deteriorate (see OECD 1996), thus potentially increasing the implicit public debt. According to some estimates (Anderson et al. 1996; IMF, 1996), in 1994, the overall figure for Czech public debt would increase to about 50% of GDP.

Bad loans, however, are not the only—and possibly not even the main—source of contingent liabilities for the public sector. As in market economies, pension systems based on a pay-as-you-go scheme have increasingly become a large burden on the budget.

One can compute the implicit pension debt by considering the entitlements of different categories of pensioners and of people currently working, discounting the future sums to obtain the present value. For instance, in the case of Hungary, the World Bank estimated that the total implicit pension debt (of both pensioners and workers) amounted in 1994 to about 250% of GDP (World Bank, 1996). In comparison with this figure, the officially measured public debt (80% of GDP) appears rather small. Figures for Hungary are much larger than those computed for advanced industrial countries. Estimates (Chand et al. 1997) for the G7 countries of the net present value of pension liabilities, over the period 1995–2050, range from values above 100% for France, Germany and Japan, between 70% and 80% for Italy and Canada, to the much lower figures for the United States (about 25%) and especially for the United Kingdom (less than 10%). Although Hungary is probably the CEE country with the highest implicit pension debt, figures for Poland would not differ very much.

Thus, taking into account contingent liabilities, the CEE countries display extremely high debt-to-GDP ratios. As a result, their room for manoeuvre on fiscal policy during transition is very limited.

Appendix: Consolidating Government and Central Bank Accounts

In the analysis of fiscal issues it is crucial to consolidate the government and the central bank accounts. The consolidation of accounts would naturally lead to shifting the focus on the dynamics of stocks and, thus, on the relation between short-term budgetary flows and medium-term fiscal sustainability, intrinsically linked to stock positions. This would, in turn, anchor inflation targets and forecasts to the underlying financing needs of the economy.

Let us start from the definition of budget deficit

$$D + iB + iC^g = C^g + B \tag{1}$$

where i is the domestic interest rate, and a dot over the variable indicates a change over time (time derivative). To consolidate the accounts of the central bank and of the government we can consider the profits or losses of the central bank.

The profits of the central bank are equal to the change of its net worth,

$$NW = iC^p + iC^g - ((1 + i^*)(1 + \hat{E}) - 1)EF^* \tag{2}$$

From the balance sheet of the central bank, we can derive the expression for its net worth, equal to its assets (credit to the government and to the private sector) net of its liabilities (foreign liabilities and base money). Taking the change of stocks we obtain the expression for the change of net worth that can be inserted in equation (2):

$$NW = iC^p + iC^g - ((1 + i^*)(1 + \hat{E}) - 1)EF^* = C^g - C^p - (EF^*) - M \tag{3}$$

Plugging (3) in (1) gives the consolidated public sector budget.

Real Versus Nominal Deficits

The nominal deficit of the consolidated public sector can be defined in terms of its source of financing as follows (adding to (3) the possibility of required reserves at the central bank, and distinguishing the holding of foreign debt by the government from Net Foreign Assets of the central bank):

$$D + i_b B + (i^* + \hat{E})(B^* E - NFA^* E) - i_p C_p = (M - i_s S) - C_p + B + (B^* E - NFA^* E) \tag{4}$$

where,

D = primary deficit of the Government
i_b = interest rate on net domestic debt
B = net public domestic debt
i^* = interest rate on foreign debt
E = exchange rate

B^* = external government debt
NFA^* = net foreign assets of the central bank
i_p = interest rate on credits of the central bank to the non-government sector
C_p = central bank credit to the non-government sector
M = base money (stock)
S = bank reserves at the central bank
i_s = interest rate on reserves

Transforming the expression in (1) in real terms (deflating by the domestic price level), we obtain the so-called 'real' or 'operational' deficit (see Buiter, 1997; van Wijnbergen 1990).

$$d + r_b B + (r^* + \hat{e})(b^* e - nfa^* e) - r_p c_p = (m + \pi m - i_s s) - c_p + b + (b^* e - nfa^* e) \quad (5)$$

Lower case letters indicate variables measured in real terms. Note that $m + \pi m$ denotes seignorage, composed of the real change in base money and the inflation tax.

Notes

1. The relation between income distribution and growth has been a 'classic' topic in economics since the contribution of Kuznets. In the old theories, the focus was on the effects of growth on income distribution. In the recent theories, the focus has shifted to the impact of income distribution on growth.
2. Since 1994, New Zealand is the country that follows more closely this approach, by preparing balance sheet accounts for the public sector.
3. This approach has been applied by the World Bank to Hungary and Romania, and by Budina and van Wijnbergen (1995) to Bulgaria.
4. Developed and developing countries included in the Barro equations, that have an average income per capita of about US $3,900, compared to the US $4,400 of the group of transition economies considered by Fischer et al. (1996).
5. The regression involves 74 countries. The dependent variable is the average rate of growth of GDP over the period 1970–85. Explanatory variables are the initial level of GDP (GDP70), government consumption (GC), social security expenditures (SS), government investment (GI) and private investment (I). The results are as follows (with standard errors below the coefficients):

   $Gr7085 = -0.000 - 0.015 \, Ln \, (GDP70) - 0.129 \, GC - 0.228 \, GI + 0.111 \, SS + 0.217 \, I$
   $\quad\quad\quad\quad\quad (0.004) \quad\quad\quad\quad (0.047) \quad (0.155) \quad (0.054) \quad (0.041)$

   $R^2 = 0.39$
6. In contrast, with the so-called Ricardian equivalence, according to which a reduction of private savings would be offset by an increase in private savings, as the public internalizes the future tax liabilities implied by the current reduction in public savings.
7. The experience of Hungary in 1994–5 is a case in point. The loosening of monetary policy brought immediate benefits to debt service, through a decline of interest rates on domestic bonds. The market reacted, however, with a large portfolio shift away from domestic financial savings, creating pressures on the exchange rate and on the domestic financial markets.
8. In such a context, a mechanical analysis attributing to malevolent governments, the reliance on the inflation tax may be highly misleading. Even when a government tries to maximize the welfare of the population it may turn out that it is optimal to use the inflation tax, rather than regular tax. This raises the issue of incentives for the government and the awareness of the public of such incentives. When using the inflation tax is optimal, it is also true that reducing the real stock of government debt via inflation is optimal.

9. The limits of sterilization policy were recognized by the authorities in the Czech Republic, who, during 1995, introduced administrative measures to curb capital inflows (fees on foreign exchange transactions between central bank and commercial banks, increases in reserve requirements and ceilings on foreign currency positions of commercial banks). Moreover, at the beginning of 1996 the exchange rate regime was modified, with the introduction of an exchange rate band (with a fluctuation band of +/– 7.5%).
10. Interestingly, only Slovenia used indexation in the financial sector to moderate the effects of stabilization policies on real interest rates. The experience seems to have been successful (Bole, 1996).
11. In addition, countries beginning transition with a sizeable monetary overhang faced the dilemma of either eliminating the overhang through a jump in the price level, or absorbing the monetary overhang by exchanging it with government assets (real or financial). The easiest example of how the monetary overhang can translate into a fiscal problem is the shift from zero rates of interest on deposits to high interest rates. The increase in interest rates would change the demand for money, and, thus, make some of the overhang a voluntary holding of monetary assets. Interest rates, however, have to be paid and, thus, the overhang transformed into a sort of interest-bearing government debt.
12. This implies, as well, that the base for inflation tax is broad money. As a result, the inflation tax would appear very large, well above the already high numbers obtained by measuring it in relation to base money.
13. Of course, considering the whole stock of bad loans as government debt sets the upper bound for such measure. Indeed, part of these bad loans could be recoverable.

6

The Fiscal Policy Stance in Central and Eastern Europe in Comparison to European Union Countries[1]

Urszula Kosterna

6.1 Fiscal Developments in EU Countries in an Historical Perspective

In the past three decades some noticeable changes have taken place in the economic policies of the developed market economies and, in particular, in the perception of the role of fiscal policy[2]. Four periods can be distinguished in the state of public finances in the EU countries (de Haan, Sterks and de Kam, 1994)—see Table 6.1.

- The 1960s, characterized by public sector expansion, resulted in a rapidly increasing proportion of budget expenditure and revenue to GDP. The growing role of the public sector reflected a general belief that the government should be involved in market processes, as well as ideas about the effectiveness and usefulness of an active stabilization policy. Fiscal policy was regarded as a key instrument in counter-cyclical demand management. The idea of the 'welfare state' influenced the structure of government expenditure; indeed, the increase in government expenditure resulted mainly from growth in social sector spending.
- The 1970s and early 1980s were a phase of a severe worsening of fiscal balances. The ratio of steady growth of budget expenditure to GDP was not compensated by an increase in revenue, even though the levels of tax rates and social security contributions were raised. As a result, there was an increase in budget deficits, which were exceptionally large in the second half of the 1970s. After 1975, public debt as a percentage of GDP, which had showed a slight downward tendency between 1960 and 1975, started to rise. The deterioration in public finances was due not only to discretionary fiscal activities, but also to a slower pace of economic growth and rising unemployment.

Table 6.1 Revenues, expenditures and general government budget balance in 12 European Union countries. In percent of GDP

	1960	1965	1970	1975	1980	1985	1990	1995
Belgium								
Revenues	27.9	31.3	39.1	45.4	48.8	52.6	48.8	50.2
Expenditures	30.7	32.7	41.7	50.9	58.1	61.3	54.2	54.9
Balance	−2.9	−1.6	−2.6	−5.5	−9.3	−8.8	−5.4	−4.7
Denmark								
Revenues	27.9	31.2	46.1	45.7	51.5	56.0	55.9	57.1
Expenditures	24.8	29.9	42.0	47.0	54.8	58.1	57.4	60.1
Balance	+3.1	+1.3	+4.1	−1.4	−3.3	−2.0	−1.5	−3.0
France								
Revenues	34.9	38.4	39.0	41.4	46.5	49.9	49.0	49.4
Expenditures	34.6	38.4	38.1	43.8	46.6	52.7	50.6	54.3
Balance	+0.4	0.0	+0.9	−2.4	0.0	−2.9	−1.6	−4.9
Germany[a]								
Revenues	35.5	36.1	38.7	43.1	45.1	46.0	43.3	46.9
Expenditures	32.5	36.7	38.5	48.6	48.0	47.2	45.3	49.3
Balance	+3.0	−0.6	+0.2	−5.6	−2.9	−1.2	−2.1	−2.4
Greece								
Revenues	21.1	23.7	26.8	22.6	25.2	28.5	32.9	37.1
Expenditures	–	–	–	–	27.6	40.2	46.8	50.3
Balance	–	–	–	–	−2.4	−11.7	−14.0	−13.3
Ireland								
Revenues	24.8	27.9	32.1	33.3	36.5	41.1	37.9	37.2
Expenditures	28.0	33.1	36.2	45.4	48.8	52.0	40.0	39.2
Balance	−3.2	−5.1	−4.1	−12.2	−12.2	−10.8	−2.2	−2.0
Italy								
Revenues	28.8	30.1	28.8	28.5	33.3	38.3	42.2	44.9
Expenditures	30.1	34.3	32.1	39.1	41.9	50.9	53.2	53.6
Balance	−1.1	−3.8	−3.3	−10.6	−8.6	−12.6	−10.9	−8.6
Luxembourg								
Revenues	31.0	33.5	36.4	49.9	55.1	58.1	–	53.6
Expenditures	29.1	31.6	33.2	48.7	55.6	50.9	–	52.0
Balance	+2.0	+1.8	+3.0	+1.1	−0.5	+7.2	+5.9	+1.6
Netherlands								
Revenues	33.9	37.3	41.2	48.7	52.5	54.4	49.9	49.6
Expenditures	33.7	38.7	42.4	51.5	56.5	58.0	55.0	53.2
Balance	+0.2	−1.4	−1.2	−2.9	−4.0	−3.6	−5.1	−3.5
Portugal								
Revenues	19.1	21.7	26.0	27.7	30.9	33.4	34.0	38.0
Expenditures	18.5	21.5	23.2	31.9	–	43.5	38.8	43.7
Balance	+0.6	+0.3	+2.8	−4.1	–	−10.1	−5.0	−5.8
Spain								
Revenues	–	–	22.1	24.4	29.9	35.2	39.5	40.9
Expenditures	–	–	21.4	24.4	32.5	42.2	43.5	46.9
Balance	–	–	+0.7	0.0	−2.6	−6.9	−3.9	−6.0
United Kingdom								
Revenues	29.9	33.0	39.8	40.0	39.7	41.3	38.8	37.5
Expenditures	32.2	35.9	37.3	44.7	43.2	44.1	40.3	42.1
Balance	−2.2	−2.9	+2.5	−4.7	−3.5	−2.8	−1.5	−4.6

[a] Up to 1990 data refer to West Germany, from 1991 to unified Germany.

Source: Annual Economic Report for 1995. European Economy No. 59, 1995.

- In the 1980s, there was a movement towards 'budget consolidation' and sounder public finances. The change in fiscal policy orientation was dictated by growing concern about the negative impact of an overly large public sector[3] and the excessive share of this sector in the redistribution of GDP. Moreover, in many countries the fiscal deficit became difficult to control, at least partially due to excessively optimistic estimates of the potential pace of economic growth. This resulted in the transformation of 'cyclical' deficits into structural ones (Muller and Price, 1984). Persistent deficits limited decision-making possibilities in the field of fiscal policy— the budget was becoming increasingly inflexible, mainly because of the growing share of public debt service costs and transfers. The change in the direction of fiscal policy also resulted in an extension of the time-frame for making policy; there is a generally accepted view that it is necessary to formulate fiscal objectives for a longer period of time (the adoption of so-called medium-term financial strategies—see Chouraqui and Price, 1984). The following new priorities of fiscal policy thus emerged:

  (a) Restraining the growth of public debt. This raised concern about the appearance of a vicious circle, in the form of increasing public debt and budget deficits, which in turn exert upward pressure on interest rates. This pressure, detrimental from a supply-side viewpoint of economic growth, has been reinforced by the restrictive course of monetary policy carried out after 1979.
  (b) Reducing the public expenditure to GDP ratio, which would permit a decrease in the tax burden and the reduction of the relative weight of the government in the economy.
  (c) Changing the structure of budget expenditures and revenues. The purpose of tax system reforms has been mainly to broaden the tax base, while at the same time lowering marginal tax rates. Reforms concerning the expenditure side were to consist mostly of reducing the share of subsidies and transfer payments.

These objectives of fiscal policy adopted in the 1980s have not, however, been achieved. The efforts to reduce budget deficits and the scope of fiscal redistribution, and to lower public debt in relation to GDP, failed. Furthermore, structural changes in government expenditures, which had occurred during this period, went in the wrong direction—in most countries there was an increase in the share of transfer expenditures and expenditures which financed public consumption. At the same time the share of investment expenditure declined. The main reason for the difficulties in fulfilling the aims of fiscal policy was public pressure to increase government expenditures, primarily those related to implementing the idea of a 'welfare state' (Oxley and Martin, 1991). The necessity of restraining the growth of internal indebtedness forced an increase in the fiscal burden.

The first half of the 1990s saw a phase of noticeable deterioration in the fiscal situation, reflected in many countries by increases in the fiscal deficit and government expenditures as a percentage of GDP. In the EU countries, the cessation of the process of fiscal consolidation has been undoubtedly associated with the adverse impact of the cyclical factor; all declarations made by fiscal authorities have shown the intention to counteract the influence of automatic stabilizers on the fiscal balances.[4]

The objectives of fiscal policy outlined in the previous decade have not changed in the beginning of the 1990s, but due to the adoption of the Maastricht Treaty provisions, they have been formally defined and treated as one of the conditions necessary to continue the process of building the EU. Within the second stage of Economic and Monetary Union (EMU), begun on 1 January 1994, further convergence of economic policy of the member states is required. As regards fiscal policy area, to ensure compliance with budgetary discipline, an excessive deficit procedure has been established. The surveillance of the budgetary situation is based on two criteria (so-called convergence criteria, contained in the Maastricht Treaty). These are:

- the annual government budget deficit should not exceed 3% of GDP, with no monetary and compulsory financing of the deficit;
- gross public debt should not exceed 60% of GDP, unless specific additional conditions are met.

Despite efforts over a decade aimed at balancing the government budget and decreasing the public debt to GDP ratio, most countries of the EU do not meet the Maastricht fiscal convergence criteria (see Table 6.2).

Both the average fiscal deficit for 12 EU countries (5.6% of GDP in 1994; 4.7% of GDP in 1995) and the average size of public debt in those countries (68.8% of GDP in 1994; 72.6% of GDP in 1995) exceed the limits. The situation in individual countries varies, however, in 1995 the economies of only four countries (Luxembourg, Ireland, Germany and Denmark) met the deficit criterion. In the remaining countries the deficit exceeds the limit, and major fiscal difficulties are faced by Italy and Greece.

The relation of public debt to GDP also varies. The convergence criterion is met by four countries (Luxembourg, France, United Kingdom, Germany). The most difficult situations are in Belgium, Italy and Greece, where the value of public debt exceeds 120% of GDP. It is worth stressing that even in countries with a relatively low ratio of public debt to GDP, this ratio increased over the period 1989–95. The main cause of this rise was a persistent budget deficit (continued debt accumulation) as well as a reduction in the pace of economic growth.

Table 6.2 Maastricht criteria and fiscal performance of European Union countries in 1994 and 1995[a]

1994			1995		
Country	Government budget balance (% of GDP)	Gross public debt (% of GDP)	Country	Government budget balance (% of GDP)	Gross public debt (% of GDP)
Luxembourg	+1.3	9.2	Luxembourg	+1.6	9.8
Ireland	−2.4	89.0	Ireland	−2.0	83.7
Germany	−2.9	51.0	Germany	−2.4	59.4
Netherlands	−3.8	78.9	Denmark	−3.0	78.0
Denmark	−4.3	78.0	Netherlands	−3.5	78.8
Belgium	−5.5	140.1	UK	−4.6	52.4
France	−5.6	50.4	Belgium	−4.7	138.7
Portugal	−6.2	70.4	France	−4.9	53.4
UK	−6.3	50.4	Portugal	−5.8	71.7
Spain	−7.0	63.5	Spain	−6.0	65.8
Italy	−9.6	123.7	Italy	−8.6	126.8
Greece	−14.1	121.3	Greece	−13.3	125.4
EU 12	−5.6	68.8	**EU 12**	−4.7	72.6

[a] Countries are ranked according to the state of their government budget balance in 1994 and 1995.

Source: Annual Economic Report for 1995, European Economy No. 59, 1995.

6.2 The Fiscal Situation of CEE Countries from the Point of View of Their Future Membership in the EU

Reported budgetary figures in five Central and East European (CEE) countries (see Table 6.3), when compared with the situation within the EU, to provide a quite comfortable picture of fiscal discipline in transition economies.

Except for Hungary, the budget deficit and public debt/GDP ratio are lower than 3% and 60%, respectively. This picture, however, can be misleading. The first obvious reason for the caution in comparisons among transition economies is the quality and comparability of statistical data. The same point applies to comparisons between transition and EU countries. In order to ensure the correctness and effectiveness of the excessive deficit procedure within the European Community, the concepts of the government budget deficit and government debt have been precisely defined, and the adjustment procedures aimed at the transformation of budgetary aggregates in individual countries' public accounts into aggregates relevant for these agreed definitions, have been prepared. In the case of transition countries, such practices do not exist. In addition, taking into account the strong incentives for officials to present a favourable picture of the economic performance of their country, one may

Table 6.3   Government budget balance and public debt in CEE countries in 1994 and 1995

1994			1995		
Country	Government budget balance (% of GDP)	Gross public debt (% of GDP)	Country	Government budget balance (% of GDP)	Gross public debt (% of GDP)
Poland	−2.2	56.4	Poland	−2.6	51.4
Hungary	−7.5	79.9	Hungary	−4.0	77.1
Czech Republic	+0.5	38.4	Czech Republic	+0.6	−
Slovak Republic	−1.3	33.0	Slovak Republic	+0.6	33.8
Slovenia[a]	−0.2	9.7	Slovenia[a]	−0.3	8.2

[a] External public debt.

Source: MultiQuery Database: A Tool for Cross-Country Comparisons. Europe and Central Asia Region. The World Bank, Spring 1996.

suspect that the government budget deficit and the value of public debt captured by the official statistical data could be underestimated. Therefore, the quality and comparability of these data must be seen as dubious.

Furthermore, the assessment of the transition countries' fiscal situation involves some crucial issues, related to the nature of transition itself, and to the prospective accession to the European Union. These are discussed below.

By signing the European Agreements, the CEE countries have declared their intentions to become the members of the Union. As a consequence, they have structured their transformation programmes in anticipation of eventual membership in the EU. The transition process in these countries is therefore the process of the preparation for accession.[5] The goal is identical—the ability to run a healthy, market economy, adjusted to EU standards. To reach this goal, the whole economic structure of the country must be reshaped. This includes the redefinition of the role and scope of the public sector during and after transition, widespread privatization, the overall reform of public finances, and the creation of financial markets. Financial markets will make possible both the efficient mobilization of private savings and their most efficient allocation, with the leading role in resource allocation being played by the private sector. Thus, financial liberalization together with the creation and development of institutions, instruments and procedures, are the core of building a stable market economy.

The reform of public finances is perceived as one of the longest lasting processes within the transformation (Tanzi, 1993b), and there is, as discussed previously, an unquestioned interdependence between fiscal policy (budgetary aggregates) and the transition process (changes in macro- and microeconomic performance of the country). Indeed, one can hardly expect a successful balanced-budget policy during the entire journey from plan to market. To the extent that fiscal imbalances reflect the costs of necessary adjustments, they may be temporarily justified. Additionally, the advancement in structural reforms is supposed to improve the future budgetary position. Therefore, the assessment of the situation of public finances in transition countries must take into account the progress toward the creation of a market-based, relatively stable and growth-generating economic system.

The same applies to the prospect of accession to the EU. Although economic eligibility criteria for the transition countries' membership of the EU have not been defined yet, it is clear that the capacity of countries to conduct economic policies implied by EU membership, the overall degree of 'marketization' of their economies, and the existence of sound macroeconomic balances, will be the most important issues. This means that the assessment of the country's 'readiness' to join the EU will not (and should not) be judged against Maastricht convergence criteria. These criteria were designed for the current EU countries as the pre-conditions for their membership in European Monetary Union in the first round of entries only. Therefore, they are not relevant for the assessment of transition (candidate) countries' prospects of joining the EU or EMU.

Furthermore, the Maastricht convergence criteria are also inappropriate as the 'benchmarks' of sound macroeconomic performance of the CEE countries. This is because of the specifics of economies in transition, where a market infrastructure, essential for the successful transformation, is only just being created. On the one hand, in such an environment fiscal imbalances (although sometimes unavoidable) may be much more dangerous than in the case of long-established market economies. On the other hand, current fiscal aggregates are supposed to change in the course of transition; thus their current levels can not be the base for future budgetary projections. An insight into these issues is given below.

The possibilities of financing the budget deficit by non-monetary means are determined by the level of financial market development together with the size of private savings. Limited savings in post-socialist economies may be a barrier to non-monetary deficit financing. Under the Maastricht Treaty, a budget deficit of 3% of GDP has been recognized as a 'safe' level, while budget deficit financing by money creation has been simultaneously forbidden. This 'safe' level value was defined for economies with a well-established market structure, where the level of money and capital market development enables the non-banking private sector to absorb newly issued public debt.[6] The situation in transition countries is quite different—financial markets are in the initial stage of formation—therefore, a budget deficit which is small by the standards of developed market economies must be perceived as a threat to the process of price stabilization in transition economies.[7] This is of particular importance given the fact that the level of inflation in these countries considerably exceeds 3% per annum (defined in the Maastricht Treaty).[8]

Table 6.4   Broad money[a] in EU and CEE Countries. Percentage share of GDP

Denmark	61.5
France	61.4
Germany	62.5
Greece	53.2
Ireland	49.6
Netherlands	84.2
Portugal	77.1
Spain	79.2
Poland	36.5
Hungary	41.1
Czech Republic	87.3
Slovak Republic	68.9
Slovenia	43.2

[a] For CEE countries, 1995; for EU countries, 1994.

Source: For CEE countries: *MultiQuery Database* (1996);
for EU countries: World Bank (1996).

A 'safe' level of the deficit must be determined, not only in relation to GDP but also with regard to the level of monetization of the national economy (the reciprocal of money velocity); this provides an indication of the potential absorptive capacity of the financial markets and of the potential inflationary effects of the fiscal deficit. Budget deficit that may look moderate as a share of GDP may be high as a share of the broad money aggregate. Its monetization will thus have a much larger inflationary consequences. As a rule, the more mature and stable the money market, the higher the monetization level. The relation of broad money to GDP in CEE and EU countries is shown in Table 6.4.

In the Czech and Slovak Republics, the levels of economic monetization are comparable with those observed in EU countries and substantially exceed the levels in remaining transition countries.[9] It is worth adding, that within the transition period the process of slow remonetization and financial deepening took place in Poland and Slovenia, while in Hungary the tendency was opposite, with the monetization level in 1995 lower by 8.2 percentage points than in 1989.

With such a low degree of monetization in Poland, Slovenia, and Hungary, the 3% criterion for the deficit-to-GDP ratio becomes inadequate; its 'permissible' or 'safe' level—from a monetary point of view—is much lower. Therefore, tighter fiscal policy is all the more needed to support disinflation in these countries.

It must be kept in mind that the government borrowing requirement is determined not only by the size of the deficit, but also by the existence of other types of obligations of a quasi-fiscal character which are in fact substitutes for government expenditure (e.g., in Poland, restructuring bonds issued by the Ministry of Finance for recapitalization of state-owned banks). Similarly, expenditure arrears, which are not reported in the government budget balance (prepared on a cash basis), constitute a hidden form of budget deficit. This problem is particularly acute in Poland, where in 1994 and 1995 substantial arrears built up; at the end of 1995, the stock of expenditure arrears reached 0.8% of GDP.[10] Such hidden forms of government liabilities must be taken into account in future fiscal projections.

There is also an important issue of contingent liabilities of the government.[11] Such liabilities are not included in government debt in EU countries because of the problem of choosing proper discount rates in the calculation of their present value. In the case of transition countries, however, contingent liabilities have greater weight, and the less advanced the overall reforms, the more heavily these liabilities weigh. This can be illustrated by the implicit pension debt of government. Another good example is offered by loan guarantees provided to inefficient state enterprises. On the one hand, if these guarantees are exercised, they will bring about budgetary costs. On the other, they distort the allocation of credit in favour of state sector, thus reducing the production and investment of private enterprises. There are still a number of different indirect forms of supporting the inefficient state sector by governments in transition countries—e.g., the tolerance of systemic non-payment (loose financial discipline) and the use of directed credit or preferential interest rates. Such practices increase actual or contingent government fiscal liabilities and, at the same time, they are clear evidence of delays in microeconomic (enterprise) restructuring.

The protection of inefficient state-owned sector through quasi-fiscal government activities adds to the problem of the banking sector's non-performing ('bad') loans. This problem is common to most transition economies, and it has not been solved yet,[12] which means the necessity to consider the costs that the budget is going to bear for this in the future.

Thus, the level of budget deficit itself, with the omission of different quasi-fiscal and contingent liabilities of the government, cannot serve as the only base for estimating the size of future public debt, and projecting its servicing costs.

The short history of domestic debt accumulation in transition countries, given the strong dynamics of this process, suggests a risk of a debt-servicing costs explosion. It should be added that the marginal cost of public debt service in these economies exceeds its average cost, which results from changes in the structure of indebtedness, in the form of a fall in the share of 'old' debt (very often with zero servicing cost or with costs below the market level) in favour of debt being assumed at market costs. Poland's case gives an insight into the debt service problem. In 1993–5 the public debt-GDP ratio declined sharply, from 64.8% at the end of 1993 to 56.4% at the end of 1994 and 51.4% at the end of 1995, mainly as the result of the fall in the external component (large-scale debt reduction granted by foreign creditors and real exchange rate appreciation). The burden of debt service payments, however, rose significantly, from 3.8% of GDP in 1993 to 5.3% of GDP in 1995, despite vigorous economic growth and lengthening of the average maturity of the domestic debt instruments.

Current budgetary tensions, resulting from the enormous burden of financing government expenditure, are the main obstacle to continuing the disinflation process. Crowding-out[13] should also be taken into consideration, with special attention given to the specific situation of the banking sector in post-socialist countries. The banks are pursuing a very cautious credit policy due to a large share of so-called 'bad debts' in their portfolios, and the poor financial standing of enterprises. One may argue that the lack of reliable borrowers, rather than government competition for financial market resources, constitutes a barrier to transforming private sector savings into credit for the economy (Oblath and Valentinyi, 1993). In other words, it is assumed here that the savings existing in the economy would be unutilized (i.e., they would not be transformed into private investment); the existence of a budget deficit allows for their utilization and sustains total demand. Those arguments, however, do not seem convincing. On one hand, it can be presumed that a balanced budget would lead to lower interest rates (nominal and real), which in turn would improve the financial standing of enterprises increasing the circle of potential borrowers. The second aspect of this issue refers to the conditions under which the banking sector operates and its relations with the government. Although in the short-run credit for the government solves the problem of investing existing bank assets, the current (and expected future) borrowing needs of the public sector can contribute to reducing the banks' interest in financing the economy (a specific type of *ex ante* crowding-out effect).

It should be added, however, that the assessment of such a crowding-out effect in the first stages of transition process should not be entirely negative. Financing the government by the banking system makes possible the maintenance of hard budget constraints for enterprises by giving banks alternative assets in which to invest, thus, counteracting a deepening of the bad debt problem. Taking a longer time perspective, however, such a crowding-out must be viewed as counterproductive.

Due to the aforementioned specific conditions of transition economies, the Maastricht fiscal criteria cannot be treated as the 'safe' ceilings of fiscal deficit and public debt. 'Low' budget deficit and public debts, as they are currently officially recorded, do not necessarily mean sound public finances. Slow progress in structural reforms, which is not fully reflected in current budgetary aggregates, poses a risk of future fiscal imbalances and constitutes a threat to macroeconomic stabilization and sustainable growth. Therefore, further progress in restructuring the economy and reducing the role that the state plays in production and resource allocation remain the main challenges for sustainable fiscal position in transition economies.

Among the CEE countries discussed in this report the most unfavourable situation is currently faced by Hungary and Poland. As fiscal difficulties, however, are a result of the pace and depth of systemic reforms, a deterioration of the state of public finances in the Slovak Republic, where the process of microeconomic restructuring seems to be delayed in comparison with the remaining countries, may be expected.

6.3   The Structure of Budgetary Expenditures and Revenues

Given the excessive degree of fiscal burden in CEE economies, it is interesting to compare their structure of budgetary expenditure and revenues with the structure observed in EU countries.

Table 6.5 indicates that post-socialist countries, in their short history of re-introducing market mechanisms, did not manage to avoid the trap in which the Western economies find themselves: the trap of the welfare state.[14] Government expenditures—almost exclusively current expenses—are financing private and public consumption. The success in a radical elimination of subsidies at the beginning of the transformation process has been accompanied by upward pressure on social spending (see Chapter 4). As a result, the reduction of overall state expenditures that occurred was smaller than was possible. Due to errors made in social policy (granting too many social privileges, an extensive system of social benefits indexation, a delay in fundamental social security system reform), government expenditures are primarily composed of social spending, with a huge share taken up by pension benefits. In all transition countries the level of government expenditures is much too excessive in relation to the level of economic development.[15] The expenditure patterns have converged towards West European levels, while the GDP gap remains wide. Government spending is high, but spending patterns cannot alter as long as the fundamental reforms of social security expenditures are not carried out.

The existing structure of budgetary revenues within EU member-states constitutes, on one hand, the result of the lengthy development of separate (national) fiscal systems under existing cultural differences and different conditions for socio-economic development, and on the other hand, the consequence of the process of the harmonization of these systems—the process accompanying the creation of the Single European Market. Since the beginning of the 1980s, measures have been taken to reform national fiscal

Table 6.5 General government expenditures in EU (1990) and CEE (1995) countries. Percentage share of GDP

	Belgium	Denmark	France	Germany
Total expenditures	**54.7**	**57.6**	**50.2**	**45.8**
Current expenditures	**52.6**	**55.3**	**46.6**	**42.3**
• Government consumption	14.2	24.7	18.3	18.5
• Subsidies	2.9	3.0	1.6	1.9
• Social security and other transfers	24.8	20.5	23.5	19.3
• Debt interest payments	10.7	7.2	3.1	2.6
Capital expenditures[a]	**2.0**	**2.3**	**3.6**	**3.5**
	Greece	**Ireland**	**Italy**	**Netherlands**
Total expenditures	**53.9**	**44.5**	**53.2**	**56.3**
Current expenditures	**51.0**	**43.5**	**48.3**	**52.3**
• Government consumption	21.9	14.6	17.4	14.9
• Subsidies	1.8	4.4	2.2	1.6
• Social security and other transfers	16.1	16.4	18.9	29.1
• Debt interest payments	11.2	8.0	9.7	6.7
Capital expenditures[a]	**2.9**	**1.3**	**4.9**	**4.0**
	Portugal	**Spain**	**UK**	**Poland**
Total expenditures	**42.7**	**41.5**	**42.9**	**49.8**
Current expenditures	**40.2**	**35.5**	**38.1**	**47.3**
• Government consumption	19.7	14.2	20.0	14.9
• Subsidies	1.5	1.6	1.1	1.8
• Social security and other transfers	10.5	16.1	13.7	21.0
• Debt interest payments	8.6	3.6	3.4	5.3
Capital expenditures[a]	**2.4**	**6.0**	**4.7**	**2.5**
	Hungary	**Czech Rep.**	**Slovak Rep.**	**Slovenia**
Total expenditures	**55.3**	**49.8**	**47.3**	**46.2**
Current expenditures	**49.9**	**42.2**	**42.3**	**43.2**
• Government consumption	18.7	18.2	14.8	7.9
• Subsidies	3.5	3.4	4.8	3.7
• Social security and other transfers	18.8	19.4	20.5	28.6
• Debt interest payments	8.9	1.3	2.2	1.5
Capital expenditures[a]	**5.3**	**7.7**	**5.0**	**3.0**

[a] Gross fixed capital formation and net capital transfers are included in capital expenditures of European Union countries.

Source: European Union countries: Oxley. Martin (1991. pp. 158–9).
Central European countries: *MultiQuery Database: A Tool for Cross-Country Comparisons. Europe and Central Asia Region.* The World Bank, Spring 1996.

systems by reducing their complexity. At the same time, the ongoing process of integrating separate national economies within the EU—under the conditions of removed barriers to the free movement of goods, services and factors of production between the countries—is contributing to an intensification of competition, and the introduction of more favourable taxation conditions.

The creation of a single market, free of restrictions on the movement of goods, requires the harmonization of VAT systems. Among the EU countries, VAT was most recently introduced (in the 1980s) in Greece, Portugal and Spain. Currently, the tax base of VAT is nearly fully harmonized across EU countries. From January 1993, the European Council adopted measures introducing a minimum standard VAT of 15%; minimal rates for the major excise taxes have also been imposed. Despite the fact that no decisions concerning harmonization of direct tax systems (personal income tax and corporate income tax), as well as the system of social security contributions, have yet been made, a tendency to equalize tax rates has been observed since the beginning of the 1980s.

The greatest divergence in the amount of budgetary revenues within EU countries concerns social security contributions (see Table 6.6), the highest share of which is observed in France (21.4% of GDP), and the lowest in Denmark (2.8% of GDP). In Denmark, however, the bulk of social contributions is financed directly from the budget, which is why Denmark has the highest ratio of direct tax revenues to GDP (above 30%) within the EU. The differentiation in revenue from social security contributions results from various degrees of state involvement in fulfilling its welfare functions and from various systems of their financing.

The CEE countries have introduced taxation systems compatible with the EU countries. Data contained in Table 6.6 point to an apparent convergence of the budget revenue structure in both groups of countries; the tax reform process was followed by the adjustment of revenue patterns towards those of high spending EU countries. In all the CEE economies, the need to finance high government spending determines tax policy, making impossible the reduction of tax rates and of the overall fiscal burden on the economy.

Even if individual income taxation is rather low in some transition economies (Czech Republic and Slovakia), this is overwhelmed by the excessive burden of social security contributions. It means that labour taxation converged to that found in EU countries with mature welfare systems. Indirect taxation is also high. Such a heavy fiscal burden on the transition economies creates a strong barrier to fast growth.

Given this excessive fiscal burden, there is no possibility of increasing budgetary revenues through an increase in tax rates. Some reserves are likely to lie in broadening tax bases and in more efficient tax administration, although these measures alone do not seem to be sufficient to restore fiscal balances. Substantial cuts in government expenditures, especially in social welfare spending, are absolutely necessary. These can be attained only by fundamental reforms of social security (particularly of pension schemes) and public services.

Table 6.6 General government current revenues in EU and CEE countries. Percentage share of GDP

	Belgium[a]	Denmark[a]	France[b]	Germany[c]
Total current revenues	**48.4**	**57.9**	**49.0**	**43.3**
• Corporate income tax	3.0	2.1	2.0	1.7
• Personal income tax	13.6	26.0	6.0	10.6
• VAT or sales tax	7.2	9.7	7.9	6.4
• Soc. sec. contributions	15.1	2.0	18.5	15.3
	Greece[b]	**Ireland[b]**	**Italy[b]**	**Netherlands[a]**
Total current revenues	**33.4**	**38.5**	**43.3**	**50.1**
• Corporate income tax	1.7	1.3	3.8	3.5
• Personal income tax	4.0	11.9	10.5	9.7
• VAT or sales tax	8.5	8.1	5.7	7.5
• Soc. sec. contributions	10.7	6.0	13.2	18.9
	Portugal[c]	**Spain[b]**	**UK[c]**	**Poland[d]**
Total current revenues	**34.0**	**40.3**	**38.8**	**46.1**
• Corporate income tax	3.2	2.7	4.0	3.1
• Personal income tax	6.3	8.1	10.4	9.7
• VAT or sales tax	6.8	5.4	6.0	12.9
• Soc. sec. contributions	9.8	11.6	6.4	11.1
	Hungary[d]	**Czech Rep.[d]**	**Slovak Rep.[d]**	**Slovenia[d]**
Total current revenues	**47.9**	**49.2**	**47.9**	**45.9**
• Corporate income tax	1.1	5.0	6.6	0.6
• Personal income tax	6.8	5.7	4.7	6.9
• VAT or sales tax	7.6	8.1	11.5	13.5
• Soc. sec. contributions	11.8	18.5	11.4	19.1

[a] Revenue shares in GDP, 1989.
[b] Revenue shares in GDP, 1991.
[c] Revenue shares in GDP, 1990.
[d] Revenue shares in GDP, 1995.

Source: European Union countries: de Haan, Sterks and de Kam (1994);
Annual Economic Report for 1995, European Economy No. 59, 1995.
Central European countries: *MultiQuery Database: A Tool for Cross-Country Comparisons. Europe and Central Asia Region.* The World Bank, Spring 1996.

Notes

1. This chapter was written with the assistance of Ryszard Petru who prepared most of the statistical information. The author represents CASE (Center for Social and Economic Research), a private international research and policy advising institution in Warsaw specializing in problems of the post-communist transition process. The author used extensively in this paper the results and conclusions of an earlier research project on 'The Fiscal Crisis in Central and Eastern Europe under Transition' carried out by CASE during the period January 1994–May 1996 and financed by the Ford Foundation. The chapter draws in particular on work done by Andrzej S. Bratkowski, Jaroslaw Bauc, Pavel Stepanek, Drahomira Vaskova, Vera Kamenickova, Vera Uldrichova, Milena Horcicova, Stefan Adamec, Antal Gyulavari, Judit Nemenyi, Lucjan T. Orlowski, Malgorzata Antczak, Marcin Luczynski, Krzysztof Polomski, Alain de Crombrugghe, Barbara Fakin, Luca Barbone, Hana Polackova, Jeffrey Sachs, and Andrew Warner. Of course, the author of this chapter takes exclusive responsibility for its content, quality, and conclusions.
2. See Chouraqui (1988), pp. 1–8; Italianer and Ohly (1994); Kosterna (1995), pp. 34–41.
3. The size of public sector—according to liberal opinion—has reached a level endangering long-term possibilities for economic growth, and at the same time has made more difficult the exercise of effective control over it. This has been described by Harris as follows: 'The private sector is a part of the economy being controlled by the government, and the public sector is a part being controlled by nobody' (quoted in Wojtyna, 1990, p. 147).
4. Only in Denmark, France and at the beginning of decade in United Kingdom, were attempts undertaken to fight recession with the help of discretionary fiscal policy. It is worth noting that the restrictive fiscal policy forced by the need to halt the growth of deficits during periods of slower economic growth operates 'pro-cyclically', thus affecting the process of overcoming the recession. This is one aspect of the reduced decision-making possibilities for fiscal policy, when the desired (from the economic perspective), softer shape of fiscal policy cannot be implemented. This dilemma of the EU countries' economic policy, at the beginning of the 1990s, is to a large degree a consequence of making only partial use of the conditions conducive to economic expansion in the second half of the 1980s, and of an excessive relaxation of fiscal policy, which resulted in a smaller than possible reduction of deficits. See Kosterna (1995), pp. 69–70.
5. This initiative could have facilitated and speeded up the process of transformation. With the broad acceptance of the idea of joining EU (especially at first stages of transition), some socially difficult and thus politically unpopular reforms (e.g., of social security system) might have been undertaken more easily, as steps required for accession. Unfortunately, this opportunity has been so far been wasted.
6. Then, both the monetary base and broadly-defined money supply are not being changed. Under conditions when the deficit is financed by the central bank, an increase in the monetary base and overall money supply occurs, but when treasury bonds are being sold to commercial banks (having free cash reserves) an increase in broadly-defined money takes place, despite the fact that the monetary base does not expand. For more information on the monetary effects of deficit financing see: Kosterna, 1995, pp. 89–93, and *Budget Financing and Monetary Control*, 1982.
7. The influence of the existing (and anticipated) budget deficit on inflationary expectations should also be taken into account.
8. In 1995, the inflation rate (average yearly increase in the consumer price index) amounted to 27.8% in Poland, 28.2% in Hungary, 9.1% in the Czech Republic, 9.9% in the Slovak Republic, and 12.6% in Slovenia. Among 12 EU countries, the highest price rises in 1994 were recorded in Greece (10.8%), Portugal (5.5%), Spain (4.9%) and Italy (4.0% of GDP). In other countries, inflation varied between 1.7% (in France) and 2.8% (in Ireland).
9. It is noteworthy that in these two countries of the former Czechoslovakia the share of domestic money in total money supply is the largest within the group of countries being examined. If one assumes that in order to measure the inflationary effects of a money supply increase, the relation of domestic money balances to GDP is important, then the situation in Poland, Hungary and Slovenia becomes even more difficult. This ratio amounted to 29.0% in Poland, 30.8% in Hungary, and 29.3% in Slovenia.

10. These expenditure arrears were concentrated in education and health care.
11. See also Chapter 5 of this report for a discussion of contingent government liabilities.
12. For more about the activities carried out within the transition countries aimed at the banking sector recovery, see Dabrowski, Mizsei and Rostowski (1995), pp. 299–300.
13. This concerns financial (indirect) crowding-out, the merit of which is absorption of private saving for financing the fiscal deficit and public debt. The competition between the private sector and the government for limited private savings leads to an increase in interest rates, which 'crowds out' private investments in favour of government expenditures. It should be noted that apart from possible financial crowding-out, direct crowding-out—being a relic of the previously existing system—also frequently occurs. This takes place when the government, through its expenditure, provides the private sector with goods and services perceived as substitutes for possible private expenditures (educational, health service expenditures, etc). Direct crowding-out does not depend on the way in which the budget deficit is financed. For more about the taxonomy of the crowding-out effect, see Buiter (1977, 1985), Chouraqui (1988), and Kosterna (1995, pp. 106–25).
14. As early as in 1958, Prof. Wilhelm Ropke, one of the authors of the German economic success wrote: 'A welfare state has a built-in inclination for further development that is impossible to be eliminated. Every now and again other sectors are being given mandatory assistance. Every now and again different groups of society become the subjects falling within the scope of that aid.' Quoted in Koronacki (1996).
15. It is worth adding that the effectiveness of government expenditures in post-socialist countries is considered to be much lower than in the majority of mature market economies. See Fakin and de Crombrugghe (1995).

7

Conclusions and Recommendations

Lorand Ambrus-Lakatos and Mark E Schaffer

7.1   Introduction

Transition has caused very specific and strong pressures on the budget of the Central and East European (CEE) countries, and large transition-specific fiscal problems remain. On the one hand, there are still budgetary costs associated with, e.g., high unemployment, bank recapitalization, and above all with the state pension system. On the other hand, the very objective of attaining fiscal and external balance is a major goal in itself for the transition. Being lenient on large budget deficits, indebtedness, or inflationary finance threatens to undermine macro stability and the coherence and success of the reforms in general. In addition, 'sound fiscal fundamentals' are prerequisites for successful institutional reforms at the micro-level. Finally, integration into the European Union (EU) requires a convergence to some appropriate criteria for macroeconomic balance.

The proper balance to strike will depend on a wide range of economic and political factors which are country-specific. Moreover, in large part because transition is 'terra nova' and forecasts and the experiences of other countries present only limited guidance for policy-making, there is a variety of views on how to strike the balance. In particular, our authors take different views of the disinflation path to aim for. Dabrowski and Kosterna are concerned that the macro stability of the CEE countries is fragile, and hence, a strong fiscal stance is necessary so that stabilization and disinflation are continued rather than endangered. Coricelli emphasises that the fiscal room for manoeuvre in the CEE countries is very limited, and the costs of rapid disinflation could be very high. These are, however, primarily differences of emphasis—there is a clear consensus on the assessment of the difficult fiscal situation and fragile macroeconomic stability in the CEE countries, on the fact that policy-makers in these countries face hard choices and strong pressures from many directions, and on the core reforms which policy-makers should aim for. In this conclusion, drawing in part on the preceding chapters by Coricelli, Dabrowski and Kosterna, we (the editors) present and discuss a selection of key measures and recommendations, with particular attention to how to link fiscal reform to EU accession.

7.2   General Conclusions and Recommendations

To begin with, the calculation and presentation of the government accounts in the CEE countries are not ideal. It would be very helpful, not just for policy-making but also for the purpose of raising public awareness of fiscal costs, if proper and open fiscal accounting were adopted. A minimal aim should be to prepare budgetary accounts in line with norms in use in the EU. The specificities of transition, however, mean that more is needed.

Continued structural change and microeconomic reform have fiscal implications—pension reform has not yet really started, unemployment will remain high in most CEE countries for some years to come, large volumes of infrastructure investment are needed, and so on. This implies extra demands on an already overburdened budget. These demands will be substantial for some years while the transition continues, hence, the notion of a 'transitional budget'. At the same time, these countries are also implementing stabilization policies in environments with 'transitional' features. Government debt levels are low in most countries but have been increasing, the contingent debt liabilities of the government are very large but prudent policy would imply their reduction; and quasi-fiscal transfers and off-budget subsidies are still sometimes large. Finally, the information presented in a clear and detailed set of fiscal accounts is valuable in a number of settings: for not just for policy-makers considering economic policy options, but also for raising public awareness of the fiscal constraints facing their countries, for all sides in the EU accession negotiations, etc.

The fiscal accounts should include regular preparation of accounts identifying the operational deficit of the government along the lines discussed in Chapter 5 of this Report. A full and open accounting of quasi-fiscal transfers and off-budget subsidies is needed. Finally, an open accounting of the contingent liabilities of the government, including above all the state pension system, is very important.

With respect to specific fiscal policy measures, this Report has argued that, first and foremost, spending reforms are critical and must be achieved, whatever balance is struck temporarily (i.e., during transition). The key fiscal time bomb is pensions—the implicit debt of the state pension system is huge, both in absolute terms and in comparison to levels in Western countries, meaning the apparently sound fiscal positions observed in many CEE countries are in fact rather bad. Other items on the policy agenda with important fiscal implications are health-care reform, reform of the education sector, and unemployment and social safety nets.

Reforms on the revenue side are also pressing, though none weigh so heavily as pension reform. The reform of the tax system has made considerable progress and the essential elements of an EU-type tax system are now in place. There remain, however, important problems. Excessively high social security tax rates, relating again to the pension problem, are one problem; the ability of enterprises to run tax arrears, essentially extracting subsidies from the state, is another.

7.3 Accession Criteria

Accession to the EU by the CEE countries is very much on the agenda now, and fiscal policy will figure in the negotiations.[1] We recommend that enactment of certain measures and achievement of certain fiscal targets should be linked to EU accession. This would benefit both the EU, by admitting countries with sounder finances, and the accession candidates, by making politically difficult fiscal reform measures more acceptable to the public.

The key requirement set by the EU for the accession candidates is that they have functioning market economies and the capacity to manage economic policy consistent with the obligations of EU member-states. For fiscal policy, this means in the first instance the ability to conduct fiscal policy with standard tools, standard revenue and expenditure categories, standard budget accounting, and so forth. The leading CEE countries have much of the above in place, though much remains to be done.

Negotiations, moreover, need to be conducted with full information available about the fiscal situation of the candidate countries. The EU should not let in countries with hidden fiscal time bombs. The implication is that accession negotiations should include a requirement from candidates to comply with the 'accounting recommendations' in section 7.2 above, in particular, presentation of the fiscal accounts in terms of the operational deficit, accounting for quasi-fiscal transfers and off-budget subsidies, and estimation of the scale of the contingent liabilities of the government. These findings should, moreover, be openly published.

The current experience of the EU member-states with Economic and Monetary Union (EMU) and the 'Maastricht criteria' raise the following question. Should there be some numerical macroeconomic criteria specified which CEE countries are asked to meet in order to be considered as candidates for EU membership, or that they must meet before being allowed in? What should these criteria be and when should they be satisfied?

We must first distinguish between criteria for entering the EU and for entering EMU. Entry to EMU is a larger issue, and applies also to current EU members who will not be entering EMU in the 'first round' and who may also wish to negotiate entry to EMU at a later date. We present specific suggestions only; on EU entry however, EMU should also be mentioned.

The fiscal and macro situations in the CEE countries are of course very different from those in the EU countries. An abrupt switch to a policy mechanism which 'suits' a member of the EU or EMU may turn out to be counterproductive. But a date should be announced when the policy in question should be phased out. All this applies to fiscal issues treated here as well: this responds to the dilemma of whether a strict compliance to the demands of the EMU should be immediately observed or some more subtle recommendation should be made. Daviddi and Ilzkovitz (1996) suggest the setting up of monitoring systems which track the management of the phase-out and the basic capacity to conduct policies consistent with EU and EMU membership. Given that CEE countries would like to become EU and then EMU members, they have to prepare to fit into the economic system of these arrangements. At that point many of their policies will cease to be independent; hence policy formulation should recognize that a large degree of policy-making independence will also be phased out.

An advantage of fixed numerical economic criteria for EU entry is that they can help build public support for, and the determination of governments to enact, otherwise unpopular fiscal reforms and macro policy. Popular opinion and politicians in the CEE countries strongly support EU entry. A danger of such criteria is that if the criteria are chosen and/or formulated poorly, countries can get into difficulties in the course of trying to meet them if, e.g., the business cycle is not favourable or unexpected developments take place.

What should these criteria be? Simply lifting the Maastricht criteria is a mistake—these were defined for a very different purpose altogether—entry into EMU by developed market economies already in the EU—and indeed do not seem to be ideally suited even for this role. They are, however, suggestive, and the experiences of the EU countries with the Maastricht criteria, both positive and negative, have influenced our suggestions below.

We have three specific suggestions for macroeconomic accession criteria: an inflation target, an upper limit for the size of government debt, and the formulation and implementation of policies to reduce the scale of the contingent liabilities of the government to an acceptable level.

1. *Inflation target.* The target of low inflation is of course very desirable in its own right. It is also worth pointing out that some incumbent EU members may object to regular and substantial devaluations required by even moderate-inflation countries. A variety of formulations is available:

under 8% per annum, say, for one year, or several years in succession. In any case, the criterion should be feasible for entrants to meet with some effort, but without having to impose excessive costs (in terms of unemployment and lost growth).

2. *Government debt.* The debt/GDP ratio is a medium-term measure with a sound economic foundation (as discussed in Chapter 5 of this Report), and is consistent with the likely emphasis in the accession negotiations on debt sustainability. We recommend an upper limit 60% of GDP. There may be some concern, however, that this 'unfairly penalizes' Hungary and Poland, which are leading transition countries but with large inherited external debt. Hence, it may be desirable to choose the upper limit of 60% of GDP for these countries, but possibly lower figures for other CEE accession candidates.

    We do not, however, believe it is desirable to set a specific target for the budget deficit. As discussed in Chapter 5, this indicator as usually measured has important shortcomings. It is, moreover, a short-term concept, a poor indicator of debt sustainability. We note here the difficulties now being encountered by some EU members in trying to meet the Maastricht budget deficit criteria at the wrong time in the business cycle.

3. *Contingent liabilities of the government.* This report has argued that reforms which reduce the contingent liabilities of the governments in Central and Eastern Europe, and in particular the implicit debt of the state pension systems, are central. We suggest that the accession candidates should be required to present, and then begin implementation, of reform programmes which will reduce the contingent liabilities of the government to levels typical of current EU member countries (an upper limit of 50% of GDP as the final objective of a convergence programme for state pension reform is one possibility). Information on the current scale of these liabilities in the CEE countries is lacking, and so we do not recommend here a firm time-scale for the actual implementation of such programmes.

Note

1. For a discussion of CEE accession generally, see Von Hagen et al. (1996). For a detailed analysis, from an EU perspective, of what will be required from the CEE candidate countries in terms of macroeconomic policies and reforms, see Daviddi and Ilzkovitz (1996).

References

Adamec, S. (1995): 'Fiscal Policy in the Slovak Republic', Center for Social and Economic Research (CASE), Warsaw, *Studies and Analyses*, No. 43.

Aghion, P. and Blanchard, O. (1993): 'On the Speed of Transition in Central Europe', EBRD Working Paper No. 6, EBRD, London.

Anderson, R., Berglöf, E. and Mizsei, K. (1996): *Banking Sector Development in Central and Eastern Europe*, Economic Policy Initiative, Report No. 1, London: Centre for Economic Policy Research and Institute for EastWest Studies.

Antezak, M. (1996): 'Income from the Privatization of State Enterprises in Poland, Hungary and Czech Republic in 1991–1994', Center for Social and Economic Research (CASE), Warsaw, *Studies and Analyses*, No. 80.

Aslund, A. (1994): 'Lessons of the First Four Years of Systemic Change in Eastern Europe', *Journal of Comparative Economics* 19, 1.

Balcerowicz, L. (1994): 'Understanding Post-communist Transitions', *Journal of Democracy* 5, 4.

Balcerowicz, L. and Gelb, A. (1995): 'Macropolicies in Transition to a Market Economy: A Three-Year Perspective', Center for Social and Economic Research (CASE), Warsaw, *Studies and Analyses*, No. 33.

Barbone, L., and Marchetti, D. J. (1995): 'Transition and the Fiscal Crisis in Central Europe', Center for Social and Economic Research (CASE), Warsaw, *Studies and Analyses*, No. 40.

Barbone, L. and Polackova, H., (1996): 'Public Finances and Economic Transition', Center for Social and Economic Research, Warsaw (CASE), *Studies and Analyses*, No. 68.

Barro, R. (1991): 'Economic Growth in a Cross-section of Countries', *Quarterly Journal of Economics* 106

Bratkowski, A. S. (1993): 'Sytuacja budzetu w Polsce w okresie transformacji' (The Situation of the Polish Budget During Transition)', Center for Social and Economic Research (CASE), Warsaw, *Studies and Analyses*, No. 10.

Bratkowski, A. S. et al. (1995): 'Fiscal Policy in Poland under Transition', Center for Social and Economic Research (CASE), Warsaw, *Studies and Analyses*, No. 49.

Bruno, M. and Easterly W. (1995): 'Is Stabilization Expansionary?', mimeo, World Bank.

Budina, N. (1997): 'Essays on Consistency of Fiscal and Monetary Policy in Eastern Europe', Ph.D. thesis, University of Amsterdam.

Budina, N. and van Wijnbergen, S. (1995): 'Fiscal Sustainability: The Case of Bulgaria', mimeo, University of Amsteram.

Buiter, W. (1997): '"Crowding Out" and the Effectiveness of Fiscal Policy', *Journal of Public Economics*, June.

Buiter, W. (1985): 'A Guide to Public Sector Debt and Deficits', *Economic Policy* 1, October.

Buiter, W. (1997): 'Fiscal Performance of Transition Economics Under Fund-Supported Programs', CEPR Discussion Paper No. 1535.

Burda, M. and Lubyova, M. (1995): 'The Impact of Active Labour Market Policies: A Closer Look at the Czech and Slovak Republics', in D. Newbery (ed.), *Tax and Benefit Reform in Central and Eastern Europe*, London: Centre for Economic Policy Research.

Calvo, G. A. and Kumar, M. S. (1993): 'Financial Markets and Intermediation', in *Financial Sector Reforms and Exchange Arrangements in Eastern Europe*, IMF Occasional Paper 102, Washington, DC: International Monetary Fund.

Chadha, B. and Coricelli, F. (1994): 'Fiscal Constraints and the Speed of Transition', CEPR Discussion Paper No. 993.

Chand, S. K. and Lorie, H. R. (1992): 'Fiscal Policy', in Vito Tanzi (ed.): *Fiscal Policies in Economies in Transition*, Washington, DC: International Monetary Fund.

Chand, S. et al. (1997): 'Ageing populations and the fiscal consequences of public pension schemes with particular reference to the major industrial countries', IMF Occasional Paper.

Chouraqui, J. (1988): 'Public Sector Deficits in OECD Countries: Causes, Consequences and Policy Reaction', in Henry Cavanna (ed.): *Public Sector Deficits in OECD Countries: Causes, Consequences and Remedies*, London: Macmillan Press.

Chouraqui, J. and Price, R. W. R. (1984): 'Medium-Term Financial Strategy: The Co-ordination of Fiscal and Monetary Policies', *OECD Economic Studies*, No. 2, Spring.

Commander, S. and Coricelli, F. (eds.) (1995): *Unemployment, Restructuring and the Labor Market in Eastern Europe and Russia*, Washington, DC: World Bank/EDI.

Coricelli, F. (1996), 'Fiscal Constraints, Reform Strategies and the Speed of Transition: The Case of Central-Eastern Europe', CEPR Discussion Paper 1339.

Coricelli, F., Hagemeier, K. and Rybibski, K. (1995): 'Poland', in Commander and Coricelli, *op cit.*

Crombrugghe, A. de (1993): 'The Polish Government Budget. Stabilization and Sustainability', Report prepared for the Institute for EastWest Studies, Namur, March.

Dąbrowski, M. (1992): 'The Polish Stabilization 1990–1991', *Journal of International and Comparative Economics* 1, 4.

Dąbrowski, M. (1995): 'Western Aid Conditionality and the Post-Communist Transition', Center for Social and Economic Research (CASE), Warsaw, *Studies and Analyses*, No. 37.

Dąbrowski, M. (1996a): 'Different Strategies of Transition to a Market Economy: How Do They Work in Practic?', World Bank Policy Research Working Paper No. 1579.

Dąbrowski, M. (1996b): 'Fiscal Crisis in the Transformation Period. Trends, Stylized Facts and Some Conceptual Problems', Center for Social and Economic Research (CASE), Warsaw, *Studies and Analyses*, No. 72.

Dąbrowski, M., Antezak, R. (1995): 'Śródła procesów inflacyjnych w Rosji, Ukrainie i Białorusi' ('Sources of Inflation in Russia, Ukraine, and Belarus'), mimeo, Instytut Nauk Ekonomicznych PAN, Warsaw, October.

Dąbrowski, M., Mizsei, K., and Rostowski, J. (1995): 'Kryzys fiskalny w krajach Europy Środkowej w okresie transformacji – studium porównawcze' ('Fiscal Crisis in Central European Countries – A Comparative Study'), in M. Dąbrowski (ed.): *Polityka gospodarcza okresu transformacji (Economic Policy of the Transformation Period)*, Warsaw: CASE – PWN.

Davvidi, R. and Ilzkovitz, F. (1996): 'The Eastern Enlargement of the European Union: Major Challenges for Macro-economic Policies and Institutions of Central and East European Countries', DGII, European Commission, paper presented at the 1996 EEA Congress.

De Gregorio, J. and Sturzenegger, F. (1994):, "Financial Markets and Inflation under Imperfect Information", IMF Working Paper 94/63.

De Haan, J., Sterks, C. G. M., and de Kam, C. A. (1994): 'An Assessment of Margins for Consolidation in the Member States of the European Union', in *Towards Greater Fiscal Discipline, European Economy: Reports and Studies*, No. 3.

De Melo, M., Denizer, C. and Gelb, A. (1996): 'From Plan to Market: The Patterns of Transition', The World Bank, Policy Research Working Paper, No. 1564.

Dewatripont, M. and Roland, G. (1992): 'The Virtues of Gradualism and Legitimacy in the Transition to a Market Economy', *Economic Journal* 102.

Dornbusch, R. and Fischer, S. (1992): 'Moderate Inflation', *World Bank Economic Review* 7, 1.

Easterly, W. and Robelo, S. (1993): 'Fiscal Policy and Economic Growth: An Empirical Investigation', The World Bank, September, mimeo.

European Bank for Reconstruction and Development (1994, 1995, 1996): *Transition Report*.

Fakin, B. and de Crombrugghe, A. (1995): 'Patterns of Government Expenditure and Taxation in Transition vs. OECD Economies', CASE – Center for Social and Economic Research, Warsaw, *Studies and Analyses*, No. 45.

Fischer, S., Sahay, R. and Vegh, C. (1996): 'From Transition to Market: Evidence and Growth Prospects', IMF Workaing Paper.

Golinowska, S. (1996): 'State Social Policy and Social Expenditure in Central and Eastern Europe', Center for Social and Economic Research (CASE), Warsaw, *Studies an Analyses*, No. 81.

Gomulka, S. (1993): 'Poland: glass half full,' in R. Portes (ed.): *Economic Transformation in Central Europe: A Progress Report*, London: CEPR and European Commission.

Gomulka, S. (1995a): 'Deficyt budżetu trzeba wyeliminował' (It is necessary to eliminate the budget deficit), *Rzeczpospolita*, 30 October 1995.

Gomulka, S. (1995b): 'The IMF-Supported Programs of Poland and Russia, 1990–1994: Principles, Errors and Results', Center for Social and Economic Research (CASE), Warsaw, *Studies and Analyses*, No. 36.

Gyulavari, A. and Nemenyi, J. (1996): 'Fiscal Policy in Hungary under Transition', Center for Social and Economic Research, Warsaw (CASE), *Studies and Analyses*, No. 64.

International Monetary Fund (1994): *World Economic Outlook* (WEO), October.

International Monetary Fund (1996): *World Economic Outlook* (WEO), May.

Italianer, A. and Ohly, C. (1994): 'Towards Greater Fiscal Discipline: An Overview', in *Towards Greater Fiscal Discipline, European Economy: Reports and Studies*, No. 3.

Kołodko, G. W. (1991): 'Transition from Socialism & Stabilization Policies: The Polish Experience', IMF Seminar Paper, Washington, DC, 11 June.

Kołodko, G. W. (1992): 'From Output Collapse to Sustainable Growth in Transition Economies. The Fiscal Implications', mimeo, Fiscal Affairs Department, IMF, December.

Koronacki, J. (1996): 'Czy państwo opiekuñeze jest dobrem?' ('Is a Welfare State a Good Thing?', *Najwyższy Czas* 3, 302, 20 January 1996.

Kosterna, U. (1995): *Deficyt budżetu państwa i jego skutki ekonomiczne* (The Budget Deficit and Its Economic Consequences), Warsaw: CASE – PWN.

Kowalik, T. (1993): 'Privatization in Poland – Social Process or Another Shock', paper presented at the International Workshop on Privatization Experiences in Eastern Europe, 21–22 May 1993.

Levine and Renelt (1992): 'A Sensitivity Analysis of Cross-country Growth Regressions', *American Economic Review* 82, 4.

MultiQuery Database (1995), prepared by Nancy Vandycke, under the supervision of Luca Barbone, the World Bank, EC2, 15 March 1995.

MultiQuery Database (1996): *MultiQuery Database: A Tool for Cross-Country Comparisions*, Europe and Central Asia Region, the World Bank, Spring 1996.

Muller, P. and Price, R. W. R. (1984): *Structural Budget Deficits and Fiscal Stance*, OECD Economics and Statistics Department Working Papers No. 15, July.

Nuti, D. M., and Portes, R. (1993): 'Central Europe: The Way Forward'. in R. Portes (ed.): *Economic Transformation in Central Europe: A Progress Report*, London: CEPR and European Commission.

Oblath, G. and Valentinyi, A. (1993): 'Macroeconomic Policy, Liberalization and Transition: Hungary's Case', Center for Social and Economic Research (CASE), Warsaw, *Studies and Analyses*, No. 8.

OECD (1982): *Budget Financing and Monetary Control*, OECD Monetary Studies Series.

OECD, *OECD Economic Surveys: The Czech Republic*, Paris: OECD, 1996.

Orlowski, L. T. (1996): 'Fiscal Consolidation in Central Europe in Preparation for Accession to the European Union', Center for Social and Economic Research (CASE), Warsaw, *Studies and Analyses*, No. 77.

Oxley, H. and Martin, J. P. (1991): 'Controlling Government Spending and Deficits: Trends in the 1980s and Prospects for the 1990s', *OECD Economic Studies*, No. 17, Autumn.

Roland, G. (1994): 'On the Speed and Sequencing of Privatization and Restructuring', *Economic Journal*, 104, pp. 1158–68, September.

Sachs, J. D. (1995a): Reforms in Eastern Europe and the Former Soviet Union in Light of the East Asian Experiences', Center for Social and Economic Research (CASE), Warsaw, *Studies and Analyses*, No. 39.

Sachs, J. D. (1995b): 'Postcommunist Parties and the Politics of Entitlements', *Transition* 6, 3, March.

Sachs, J. D. and Warner, A. M. (1996): 'Achieving Rapid Growth in the Transition Economies of Central Europe', Center for Social and Economic Research (CASE), Warsaw, *Studies and Analyses*, No. 73.

Sala-i-Martin, X. (1996): 'A positive Theory of Social Security', *Journal of Economic Growth* 1.

Schaffer, M. E. (1995): 'Government Subsidies to Enterprises in Central and Eastern Europe: Budgetary Subsidies and Tax Arrears', in: D. M. Newbery (ed.): *Tax and Benefit Reform in Central and Eastern Europe*, London: CEPR.

Stepanek, P. et al. (1995): 'Fiscal Policy in the Czech Republic under Transition', Center for Social and Economic Research (CASE), Warsaw, *Studies and Analyses*, No. 51.

Tanzi, V. (1993a): 'The Budget Deficit in Transition', *IMF Staff Papers* 3.

Tanzi, V. (1993b): 'Financial Markets and Public Finance in the Transformation Process', in V. Tanzi (ed.), *Transition to Market: Studies in Fiscal Reform*, Washington, DC: International Monetary Fund.

Uldrichova, V. (1996): 'Current Problems in the Financing of the Czech Public Health System', Center for Social and Economic Research (CASE), Warsaw, *Studies and Analyses*, No. 83.

Van Wijnbergen, S. (1990): 'External Debt, Inflation and the Public Sector: Towards Fiscal Policy for Sustainable Growth', *World Bank Economic Review 3*.

Vaskova, D. (1996): 'Comparison of the Tax Stucture in CE and EU Countries: Tax Reform Goals and the Current Situation', Center for Social and Economic Research (CASE), Warsaw, *Studies and Analyses*, No. 82.

Von Hagen, J., Kumar, A., and Kawecka-Wyrzykowska, E. (1996): *Coming to Terms with Accession*, Economic Policy Initiative, Report No. 2, London: Centre for Economic Policy Research and Insitute for EastWest Studies.

Wierzba R. (1993): 'Obciążenia fiskalne w Polsce na tle krajów członkowskich Wspólnoty Europejskiej' ('Fiscal Burdens in Poland in Comparison with Member Countries of the European Community'), *Bank i Kredyt*, No. 11.

Wojtyna A. (1990): *Nowoczesne państwa kapitalistyczne a gospodarka. Teoria i praktyka* (Contemporary Capitalist State and Economy: Theory and Practice), Warsaw: PWN.

World Bank (1995): 'Workers in an Integrating World', *World Development Report* (WDR), Washington, DC: World Bank.

World Bank (1996a): 'From Plan to Market', *World Development Report* (WDR), Washington, DC: World Bank.

World Bank (1996b): *Hungary: A World Bank Country Study*, Washington, DC: World Bank.

Index

accession 58–9, 70–3
active labour market policy (ALMP) 32
adjustment of revenue 7
administration of tax 37, 65–6
Agreement on Monetary, Economic and
        Social Union 3
agricultural sector 11
Albania 3, 7–9
allocation of resources 24–5, 63
Ambrus-Lakatos, L. 1–2, 69–73
armed conflict 4
Armenia 4
arrears
    expenditure 61
    tax 30, 71
autarky 4
Azerbaijan 4

bad loans 48–9, 61–2
Baltic countries 13
banking 4, 48–9, 61–2
Barro equation 43
base money 39–40
Belarus 4, 13
Belgium 56
bonds 45
borrowing requirements 60–1
Bosnia 4
Brezhnev, L. 5
broad money 60
budget deficit 6–7, 14, 39
    accession criteria 73
    control 55
    debt 57
    EU 56
    financing 59–60

growth 44–5
indicators 16, 17
nominal 41–2, 50–1
operational 41, 42
real 41–2, 50–1
size 39, 43–9
subsidies 30
budgets 4, 16–23, 55
    expenditure 55, 63–6
    redistribution 27–8
    revenue 5–6, 14
    subsidies 12
Budina, N. 42
Buiter, W. 41
Bulgaria 4, 7, 8, 9
    debt 5, 12, 46
    deficit 41–2
    fiscal crises 13
    profit tax 21

Canada 49
capital
    expenditures 8–9
    sterilization 47–8
    stock 18
central banks
    account consolidation 41, 50–1
    bonds 47
    quasi-fiscal spending 6
centralization 4, 5, 24
Chile 27
Chouraqui, J. 55
command-and-distribute economies 24
commercial banks 45, 47
compensation packages 24
competition 10

concessionary loans 7
consistency 3
consumption 63
contingent liabilities 48–9, 61, 73
convergence 56, 59, 73
Coricelli, F. 16–23, 39–52, 69, 70
corporate income tax 37, 65
costs 17, 18, 21
 debt 55, 61
 unemployment 69
credit 44–5, 62
Croatia 3, 10, 14
crowding-out 39, 44, 47, 62
currency inconvertibility 4
Czech Republic 3, 9
 corporate income tax 37
 debt 48–9
 EU accession 1
 expenditure 28
 fiscal consolidation 14
 fiscal crises 12–13
 income tax 65
 inflation 47
 monetization 60
 pensions 31
 revenue 25–6, 36–7
 unemployment benefits 33
 VAT 10
Czechoslovakia 5, 6, 9
 debt 46
 fiscal adjustment 7, 8
 revenue 34
 unemployment benefits 32

Dąbrowski, M. 3–15, 69, 70
Daviddi, R. 72
debt 5, 12, 53, 73
 accumulation 61
 deficit 39, 40, 57
 dynamics 45–7
 financing 39
 implicit 48–9
 implied targets 41
 interest payments 33
 service costs 55
defence spending 6
deficit see budget deficit
demand management 53
Denmark 56, 65
deposits 48–9
destabilization stage 4–6
devaluation 46, 72
Dewatripont, M. 21
disability pensions 11, 31
disinflation 62, 69
duplication effect 10

East Asia 28, 31
Economic and Monetary Union
 (EMU) 56, 71–2
education 24, 71
emergency taxes 6
employer social security contributions 37
employment liberalization 17
enterprise profit tax 10
Estonia 3, 12–14
European Agreements 58
European Council 65
European Monetary Union 59
European Union (EU)
 accession 1–2, 71–3
 enlargement 27
 fiscal policy stance 53–72
 integration 16, 69
 revenue 37
exchange rates 7, 41, 62
excise taxes 10, 65
expenditure
 adjustment 7
 arrears 61
 government cuts 6
 growth 43
 investment 44
 redistribution 39
 reduction 55
 revenue 39, 53
 structure 28–33, 63–6
 taxes 16
 welfare state 63

fast reform 3–4, 19
Federal Republic of Germany 3
financial markets 58, 62
Finland 13
firms 17
fiscal policy
 comparative analysis 24–38
 consolidation 4, 14
 constraints 19–22
 destabilization 4
 development dynamics 3–15
 disequilibrium 5
 long-term view 39–52
 redistribution 5, 24–8
 secondary crisis 9–13
 stance 53–68
foreign credits 5
foreign grants 7
France 13, 49, 56, 65

Georgia 4
German Democratic Republic (GDR) 3, 5, 6
Germany 49, 56

Gierek, – 5
governments
    account consolidation 41, 50–1
    bonds 45, 47
    borrowing requirement 60–1
    debt 73
    expenditure cuts 6
    size 24–8, 43–9
    spending 26
Greece 56, 65
Group of Seven (G-7) 49
growth
    budget deficit 39, 43–9
    expenditure 53, 55
    interest rates 40
    long-term 48–9
    sustainable 63
    taxation 65

health care 24, 33, 71
Herzegovina 4
holidays 24
Honecker, E. 5
Hong Kong 27
housing 24
human capital 43–4
Hungary 3, 6, 9
    budget 14
    central bank 41
    corporate income tax rates 37
    debt 5, 12, 33, 46, 48
    deficit 7, 57–8
    EU accession 1
    expenditure 28, 44
    fiscal adjustment 7–8
    fiscal costs 21
    fiscal reform 63
    government debt 73
    health care 33
    inflation 47, 48
    monetization 60
    pensions 11, 31, 49
    revenue 25–6, 34–7
    transfers 30
    unemployment benefits 32
    VAT 10
    welfare spending 13
Husak, – 5
hyperinflation 1, 8

Ilzkovitz, F. 72
incomes 17, 22
indexation 6, 11, 63
indicators 16, 19
inflation 5–7, 39, 59
    deficit 45
    target 42, 72–3

tax 34, 40, 42, 46
infrastructure 59, 70
initial destabilization stage 4–6
initial stabilization/liberalization package 6–9
Institutions 3, 24, 58
insurance 32, 37
interest rates 7, 33, 40–1, 50–1
investment 4, 6, 70
    expenditure 44
    growth 39
    social security systems 43
Ireland 56
Italy 13, 37, 49, 56

Japan 49
Jaruzelski, – 5

Kadar, – 5
Kazakstan 4
Khrushchev, N. 5
Kosterna, U. 24–38, 53–68, 69–70
Kyrgyzstan 3

labour market 17–18, 21, 32
Latin America 31
Latvia 3, 14
Levine equation 43
liberalization 3–9, 17, 28
Lithuania 3
London Club 46
Luxembourg 56

Maastricht Treaty 40, 56, 59, 62, 71–3
Macedonia 3
macroeconomics
    accession criteria 71–3
    deficit 39
    destabilization 4
    equilibrium 6
    performance 59
    stabilization 3, 63
Malaysia 27
manufacturing subsidies 24
market institutions 17
marketization 59
Mauritius 27
microeconomics 61, 70
Moldova 3, 7
monetization 60
money creation 39
monitoring systems 72
monopolies 4, 7, 10

nationalization 4
New Yugoslavia 4
New Zealand 40
non-wage benefits 24

off-budget subsidies 70, 71
output 45
overshooting 12

paper profits 10
Paris Club 46
pensions 6, 11, 17, 43
  benefits 63
  expenditure 20
  income redistribution 22
  insurance 37
  liabilities 48–9
  reform 23, 44, 66, 70–1
  targeting 21
  unfunded 30–2
  West Europe 13
Personal Income Tax Act 10
personal income tax (PIT) 34, 37
Poland 1, 3, 5, 9, 12
  consolidation 14
  corporate income tax rates 37
  debt 46, 48, 61–2, 73
  deficit 41–2
  expenditure 28–30
  fiscal adjustment 7–8
  fiscal costs 21
  fiscal reform 63
  inflation 47
  interest payments 33
  money velocity 6
  pensions 11, 31
  remonetization 60
  restructuring bonds 61
  revenue 25, 34–7
  tax proceeds 10
  unemployment benefits 32
  VAT 10
  welfare spending 13
Portugal 65
post-stabilization fiscal crisis 4
Prague Spring 5
Price, R.W.R. 55
prices
  distortions 8
  liberalization 6, 28
  regulation 4
  stabilization 59
privatization 3, 12, 13, 58
production costs 4
productivity 44
profits 4, 5
  monopolies 10
  tax 19, 21, 34
public finance reform 58–9
public sector 19, 39, 41
  composition 48
  expansion 53, 55
  inflation 45

redefinition 58
public transport 24
purchasing power parity (PPP) 27

quasi-fiscal spending 6, 30, 70–1

reallocation of resources 17
recommendations 69–73
remonetization 60
Renelt equation 43
reserve requirements 47
resources
  allocation 24–5, 63
  public sector 41
  reallocation 17
restructuring 3, 16–23, 61
retirement 11, 18, 19, 22
revenue
  adjustment 7
  distribution 20, 21
  expenditure 39, 53, 55
  structure 33–7, 63–6
Roland, G. 21
Romania 4, 30, 41, 42, 46
Russia 4

Sachs, J.D. 27
Sala-i-Martin, X. 43
savings 4, 28, 31, 62
  growth 39
  mobilization 58
  social security systems 43
Schaffer, M.E. 1–2, 69–73
secondary fiscal crisis 7, 9–13, 14
securities markets 47
seignorage 39–40
shock therapy 12
Singapore 27
Single European Market 63
Slovak Republic 3, 9, 10
  corporate income tax rates 37
  EU accession 1
  expenditure 28–30
  fiscal consolidation 14
  fiscal reform 63
  health care 33
  income tax 65
  monetization 60
  pensions 31
  revenue 25–6, 36–7
  unemployment benefits 32
  welfare spending 13
Slovenia 1, 3, 10
  expenditure 28
  fiscal consolidation 14
  fiscal crises 12
  inflation 47
  pensions 31

Slovenia—*contd.*
 remonetization 60
 revenue 25–6
 transfers 30
 unemployment benefits 32
 VAT 10
 welfare spending 13
social security systems 5, 43, 53, 63
 contributions 37, 65
 expenditure 18–22
socialist market reforms 5
South Korea 27
Spain 65
stabilization 6–9, 53, 59, 63, 70
Stalin, J. 5
state-owned enterprises (SOEs) 5, 13, 20–1, 61
states 5, 16
step-inflation 46
sterilization of capital inflows 47–8
stocks 41, 50–1
structural distortions 4
subsidies 6, 8–10, 12, 28–30
 elimination 13, 63
 hidden 41, 50–1
 incentives 17
 indicators 19
 manufacturing 24
 off-budget 70, 71
 reduction 18, 19, 21
sustainability factors 39–42
Sweden 13

Taiwan 27
Tajikstan 4
taxation 10, 33–7, 55
 arrears 30, 71
 avoidance 10
 compatibility 65
 evasion 37
 exemptions 6
 expdeniture 16
 growth 39
 rates 6, 53
 SOEs 20, 21, 22
Thailand 27

time-frames 55
trade policy 4
trade-offs 22
transfers 39, 43, 55, 70–1
transition
 fiscal development dynamics 3–15
 phases 16–23
Turkmenistan 4
turnover tax 10, 34

Ukraine 4, 13
Ulbricht, – 5
unemployment 11, 12, 71
 benefits 17–19, 21–2, 32
 costs 69
 privatization 13
 rise 53
Unification Treaty 3
Union of Soviet Socialist Republics
  (USSR) 5–6
United Kingdom (UK) 49, 56
United States of America (USA) 13, 49
Uzbekistan 4

value added tax (VAT) 10, 14, 34, 37, 65
Van Wijnbergen, S. 41
Visegrad group 13

wages 5–6, 12, 19
Wagner's law 26
Warner, A.M. 27
wealth levels 27
welfare state 30–1
 crises 27
 expenditure 53, 55, 63
 spending 5, 11–13
West Europe
 budgetary redistribution 27
 convergence 48
 pensions 13
 welfare state 63
World Bank 49

Yugoslavia 5, 6